The History of
Loch Morlich Hostel

by
John Rosenfield

Published by Coylum Publishing
Layout by Janice Rosenfield
Cover Design By A4 Print, Inverness
Printed by Berforts Press, Stevenage **www.berforts.co.uk**

ISBN 978-0-9565055-3-8

Dedication

This book is dedicated of course to my dear uncle and aunt, Dennis and Patricia. It was because of the love which they constantly showed me that I was able to lead such an idyllically happy and carefree life for all those wonderful years. It was also because of the loving care and attention they gave to the day to day running of the hostel that thousands of people came to regard it as a very special place.

That is why I thought this wonderful story deserves to be told, so that it can take its special place in the history of Glenmore.

By the Same Author

Rosenfield's Fairfax: A two-volume biography of the English Civil War General, the Commander of the New Model Army who defeated the King at the Battle of Naseby.

Paperbacks are in the Author's possession, and available by post. The electronic version is published by Oak E-Books, www.oakebooks.com/authors/

The ISBN for Vol.1 is 978-0-9565055-0-7

The ISBN for Vol.2 is 978-0-9565055-1-4

The **Forest Loch and Mountain** series of walks books.

These include (so far) The Green Loch, Around Loch Morlich, and The Coire of the Snows.

Paperbacks are in the Author's possession and available by post.

The series is published by Kobo books, and are therefore available to download and read on most devices.

One website covers all these and future books. Please see

www.spanglefish.com/coylumpublishing

Foreword

There is precious little information available about the earliest days of the shooting lodge, even from the records of the Dukes of Gordon. Tom Stevens wrote briefly about it in his 'History of Glenmore' in 1979, a booklet intended, "for the staff of Glenmore Lodge who wish to know a little more about the history of the glen, one of the most picturesque in the whole of Scotland in which the Lodge is situated." This booklet is in the author's possession.

A general history of the entire parish, 'In the Shadow of Cairngorm' was written by William Forsyth. MA, DD in 1899. The book has been re-printed and is available in bookshops, ISBN number: 1-901201-14-7.

In 1952 Catherine Loader wrote: 'Cairngorm Adventure at Glenmore Lodge' which she addressed to, "The Young People of All Countries", and wrote, "May you learn to enjoy the thrills and adventure of life in the open air, and to realise that in your hands you hold a sacred trust; the heritage of the hills and the country to which you belong." The book is available to borrow from Aviemore Library.

A chance here for me to express my heart-felt thanks and deep gratitude to IDS Thomson, who helped me so much when I began to write this book, and who himself wrote 'A History of Glenmore Lodge' covering the period from 1947 to 1960 when SYHA took over the buiding. This was published as an e-book by the Scottish Mountaineering Trust in 2003, it has an ISBN: 0-907521-82-7 and is available from: ebooks@smc.org.uk.

The Prologue

They built it, or so I have always imagined, as a shooting lodge for the Dukes of Gordon. It is no part of my task here to tell you about those fine gentlemen, but I must remark upon what a fine, and indeed spectacular site they chose. It's distinctive shape is visible from nearly anywhere in the northern Cairngorms; white, set amidst countless evergreen trees, and close by, the steely blue of Loch Morlich.

It sits on a small ledge of flat ground, a little way up the steep, south facing slope of the 'Shepherd of Glenmore', Meall a' Buchaille. The garden, between the hostel and the road, is quite steep, and for many years the gateway to the path up towards the hostel was deliniated by two tall cypress trees.

Many guide books have been written about the Cairngorms, and a word which is common to almost all of them, when describing the setting of Loch Morlich Hostel is: 'grandeur'. Indeed, the view looking outwards from the hostel towards the majesty of the Cairngorm mountains, is nothing less than grand. The graceful rounded summit of Cairngorm itself, contrasted with the sharp, glacial ridges of the northern corries is a view which spans time itself.

And more than that, as the sun journeys across those mountains each day, and as the seasons themselves change, it is the constantly variable light which impresses those who gaze upon it's beauty. That is precisely why artists, poets and photographers feel a need to return to Glenmore, and why countless thousands of holiday-makers regard it as somewhere special, even if they are not so acutely aware of it. Sometimes, in late summer, the sinking sun in the west can paint those corries a vivid red colour for a few precious minutes, and can paint the sky with more shades of pink and purple than you could possibly imagine.

This also explains why, for so many years, I was content to sit on 'my' window-sill in the hall of the hostel, simply delighting in watching the light change, either across the mountains or, (in the early days when the trees were not so tall) looking down to Loch Morlich itself. In springtime, it was the infinitely variable shades of green which never ceased to amaze me, and fascinate me still.

This day, however, is a very special day, and it finds me, as usual, sitting on my window-sill, but for quite different reasons. Today we have invited some very special guests to dinner.

The large kitchen table served us so well for all my time at the Hostel; I cannot tell how old was the original one, perhaps it came from the old Glenmore Lodge, or perhaps my Aunt brought it with her, but it always was a gathering-point for staff, family and visitors. On this day of days, on that table is laid out a great feast, a veritable banquet. Our special guests are invited to partake of that feast on one condition only: that each must tell their story, of how their deeds brought life into the old shooting-lodge, of what part they played in the history of Loch Morlich Youth Hostel.

The Norwegians' Tale

I am apprehensive as our first two guests arrive. Older gentlemen, but their straight backs and general bearing betray an unmistakeable military background. Reverently, they bow and introduce themselves. "Hallo, my apologies, my friend speaks no English, and I speak only a little. May we look round, please?" As if by way of explanation, he straightens himself, stands almost to attention, and declares: "We were soldiers in Kompani Linge."

I welcome them as most honoured guests. They gaze around the hall, open the door to the common room, and shake their heads in wonder. "Ah", says one to me, "may we please go up the stairs?" At the top, they turn to the right, looking relieved to recognise something. "Please, what is in there?" "That is the Warden's quarters, my Uncle and Aunt's flat", I reply. "Then, please may we open the door? We will not go in." I bid them welcome.

A look of pleased recognition on both their faces. "This," he announces, "was the radio room. From here we could talk to all our comrades out on the mountains. Our Lieutenant, Norman Gabrielson was in command of wireless telegraphy on Cairngorm."

They moved along the corridor, and took me into the first room on the left, which we knew as, 'F Dorm', or 'Fiacaill'. "Here is where we gathered; it was so cold sometimes", he smiled, "but we lit such a warming fire." "As far as I know", I replied, "there was never a fireplace in here." He moved to the window, opened it, and bade me look outside and upwards, to the right. There, on the roof, just above 'F Dorm', there was a chimney.

The sound of footseps in the hall brings us back down the stairs. Two more commandos have arrived. The comrades-in-arms greet each other warmly. They turn, respectfully, to address me. "Sir, Thank you for inviting us. This is the second time we have returned here since the war." In response to my surprise, he explains: "We came first in 1973, on Wednesday, 19 September, for the unveiling of the memorial." "So you did", I reply, "I remember that we were asked to provide a buffet lunch for a great party of dignitaries; we could supply the food, but we had not sufficent crockery or glasses, so I was despatched to the Aviemore Centre to borrow some more."

"It was a day of great importance", explained the commando, "for both our countries. During the war, most of us stayed in the wooden huts which were in the hostel garden. When those were taken down, it was decided to build a memorial; an opportunity for you to remember us, and for us to express our thanks to you." "It is a large stone, inscribed with the badge of Kompani Linge, and it bears the words: 'Dere åpnet deres hjem, og deres hjerter for oss, Og gav oss håp.' 'You opened your homes and your hearts to us, and gave us hope'."

"Then may I respectfully say to you, Sir," I replied, "that, in my opinion, that is a tremendous testament to the good folk who lived in and around this Glen during the war years; and a tribute to all of you comandos who displayed a loyalty and a courage which is quite beyond my capacity even to imagine."

"Thank you", another replied, "but that September day was also a day of great celebration. Those of us who came brought our wives, and we dressed for the occasion in our traditional costume; and the buffet lunch was splendid. Major Cameron Robertson, MBE attended, and the Stone itself was unveiled by Lieutenant-General Reider Kvaal, MC NATO, the Commander of Allied Forces, North Norway."

"And on that same day, we brought with us a very special bottle, a very old bottle of brandy, with an eagle on the label, German brandy. My friend here and I broke into a German airfield to sabotage the bombers there. I climbed into a Heinkel, and put a bomb under the pilot's seat; but first I found this bottle there, so I thought I would take it with me. Truth to tell, there were three of us in that group, and escaping from the airfield, our comrade was shot and killed. It was in his memory that we drank the brandy, and very fine it was. I do confess, it is a grave story, of a brave subject."

"On 9 April 1940 Nazi Germany invaded Norway; on 9 June of the same year, with his Government-in-exile in London, the Norwegian King, Haakon VII made a broadcast to his people. He said that they were all, 'determined to use all our strength, our life, and all we possess in Norway's cause.' He hoped that they might come back to a free and independent Norway with honour, and said that their task was, 'to preserve the constitutional foundations of the country and the people so that, in the hour of victory, our fatherland can arise and assert its natural freedom.' That message inspired many people, and so began what Norwegians call the 'Englandsfarere': thousands of men and women escaping from their occupied homeland to Britain. They came, almost all these ordinary men and women, in fishing boats across the North Sea; and we know that at least 18 of those boats were lost. Yet still they came; and then some units of the Norwegian Navy and the Royal Navy combined to help them. All of them shared the same hope: that they would fight to bring their King his victory with honour.

Refugees with a military background, not just from Norway but from all over occupied Europe, would inevitably have visited the Royal Patriotic School at Wandsworth; this provided a most valuable resource for British Intelligence. Two such were Captain Boughton-Leigh and James Lawrence Chaworth-Musters Lt RNVR. Both men were part of the Norwegian Section staff and were based in Norway. Chaworth-Musters was a zoologist by profession, and had identified and named 'Muster's Benghazi Mouse', (a possible derivation for the term, 'Desert Rat'.)

We have an account of Chaworth-Muster's escape from occupied Norway: "We called at the house of Ivor Berge; he gave us a map and a compass, and stuffed a leg of mutton into one of my large overcoat pockets and a loaf of bread into the other. We left about noon and made our way south to Nesttun. Germans were already on the roads, so we trekked cross-country, reaching the outskirts at about 5am. We were shelterd by some Norwegians, and within three months, we were ferried across the North Sea to England in small Norwegian boats."

His nickname with his men was, 'Submarine Cook', and before his escape he had farmed at Nordmore. He was therefore a neighbour as well as a friend of our leader, Martin Jensen Linge. Martin was born on 11 December 1894, and had taken his name from the family farm at Linge, in Nordal, north-western Norway. He graduated from the military school at Trondheim, and became interested in the theatre there. He appeared in both theatre and films between the wars. He was involved in fighting as soon as Germany invaded, and was wounded in a rearguard action at Åndalnes.

When he came to London and to Wandsworth, he was re-united with Captain Boughton-Leigh and Lt Chaworth-Musters; together, they were asked to set up and choose men for a special military unit, under the umbrella of Winston Churchill's Special Operations Executive. These Norwegian volunteers were to undergo special training in mountain warfare, in order to wage war in their German-occupied homeland; the wild remoteness of the Cairngorm mountains made it an ideal place for such training, being so similar to our homeland's terrain. Bases were set up all over Glenmore, at Drumintoul Lodge, at Forest Lodge and of course at this Youth Hostel, which we knew as Glenmore Lodge. Our hospital was based at Coylum House. Under Churchill's scheme, we were known as 'STS 26' but we preferred 'Norwegian Independent Company 1'.

Joachim Rønneberg had this to say about Martin Linge: "He was a man of great charisma and great fighting spirit, and was an inspiring leader. I had no reservations about joining up when Linge was our leader." In March 1941, Linge led a group of his soldiers as part of a British military expedition to the Lofoten Islands.

In June 1941 both men went together to set up another training school at Meoble Lodge, near Arisaig.

From there, Linge went back to London. He insisted on leading some of his men in a British combined operation to Måløy, against German military positions on Vøgsøy Island. The British called this 'Operation Archery'. "The British could not stop him, and he never came back", added Rønneberg.

"Perhaps the saddest day of the whole War for us was 1 February 1942. In Trondheim, armed Nazi police prevented thousands from attending a communion service in the Cathedral. In the church in Aviemore, quietly and with great dignity, Pastor Alf van der Hagen, Chaplain of the Seamen's Mission in Liverpool, conducted the funeral service for Martin Linge. We began with silent prayer, then we sang the Norwegian National Hymn, then some readings and a short address. After the Benediction we sang our National Anthem. They awarded our Captain Norway's highest military honour, the War Cross with Sword, and he was buried with honour in his homeland. Today streets bear his name in seven Norwegian cities, including Stavanger and Oslo, and his statue stands in Linge Park, Måløy.

But from that day forth, and now forever, we shall ourselves be known to the world as 'Kompani Linge'."

"We were not always so sad", said the other soldier. "We trained hard, as we had to in order to carry out sabotage operations. We used the beach at Loch Morlich for explosives training, and we spent days and nights on the high mountains, we built our own stone shelters on Ben Macdui. You may say it was a mixture of PT, military instruction, fieldcraft, weapons training and silent killing; irregular, but very useful methods for putting an enemy out of action."

"And we ate rather well, considering it was wartime", said his companion. "Your garden may be quite steep, but in the summer we grew potatoes and vegetables in it. In Britain you called it 'Dig for Victory'; so did we. At Badaguish there was a croft with two cows; we got some vegetables and our milk from there. There was venison, of course. Poaching was popular, but the gamekeepers knew their job, so from time to time poachers were taken. Once the Glenmore Gamekeeper came to us red-faced with anger. He explained to our commander that he had just been shot at by "a Norwegian, small with a big nose, a long knife and big feet - just like a chicken". The description was so good that everybody knew who it was. The culprit's name was Storhaug. He was immediately given the nickname 'Kyllingen' (the chicken) and he had to pay his fine. Colonel Wilson then applied to the Government for us, and we were given permission to shoot 14 deer that winter, but accompanied by the gamekeeper. It did not suit our boys to be under supervision, so poaching carried on, and twice a week privates and officers had venison for dinner. Nothing was said, but if the gamekeeper did take someone, he reported it to the commander; there was a terrible row and another fine for the poacher."

"Our recreation, when possible, was at Grantown. There was a cinema, bars, and also a dance every Friday and Saturday. During these weekends, Mammy in Grantown was very central. At Mammy's the boys had their regular place. She took good care of us Norwegians and could well have adopted the whole outfit. She knew at what time the cars with soldiers on leave would arrive from Forest or Glen, and she did things accordingly. She would close her little cafe and had an open house in her flat on the first floor. The kitchen table was full of all kinds of good food. You would hardly find such things elsewhere; bacon, eggs, raisin bread, waffles and cookies, and plenty of jam. Mammy was interested in them all; she would repair uniforms and take care of washing and cleaning. Sometimes she was worried when asking about those boys who had been sent home. She was probably the only one in town who knew anything about our work. It is possible that the security people found it useful to let her understand. She could not help hearing the talk between the boys, and draw her own conclusions when they returned after a year of absence with new medal ribbons on their breasts."

"Security, of course, was an issue right through the war. It did not help matters when some of our boys at Forest Lodge were training dressed in captured German uniforms, and someone spotted them and took a photograph."

"Quite so," I replied, "and there is a story I can tell you in return, as it was told to me by Brian Matthew. His father Ernie was in No 4 Commando, based at Braemar. Some of them, like you, were sent out on exercise from a training camp at Devil's Point. They were training to move quickly over quite large distances around the mountains. On one occasion they ran into some of your boys, and you marched them at gunpoint back here until identities were confirmed."

"You could be certain of nothing", replied the soldier. "Someone just as famous as Mammy was our Nurse, 2/Lt RNA Ingebjørg Skoghaug. She had served with the Royal Norwegian Nursing School in Edinburgh, before coming to Glenmore. She was the doctor's assistant there, and everybody's friend. From 1942 she had her office at Coylum Cottage, near Drumintoul. She was called, 'Nørsa' by everyone."

"Yes", said the other man, "her story is a very brave one too. She was born in Bergen in 1912. When war came, she escaped in one of the small boats. She sailed from Bremnes on 28 September 1941 on the M/S Utnøring, along with two other boats, the M/S Valburg and the M/S Knut. Those two were lost in a horrendous storm, but her boat had 22 people on board, including three women, and they all arrived safely at Lerwick on 30 September."

"She returned in 1973, in company with the surgeon who worked with her, and they were entertained to tea in the garden by Ann Hedley, who lives in Coylum House to this day. She wrote a letter of thanks:

'It was so nice to see Scotland again and to return to my old well known parts of your country. Especially I took pleasure in seeing Coylum House once again, the place I spent three and a half years during the war. I forward a little ring in memory of my last visit of Coylum House, and for your kind hospitality and the nice cup of tea you gave us. Thank You very much.

Yours Sincerely Ingebjørg Skoghaug (Norwegian Nurse)."

"We ought not to forget our King", said the first soldier. "Indeed not," said the second. "His Majesty was gracious enough to pay us several visits during the war, and with Crown Prince Olav. But I do not think that any of us could forget his visit in July 1943. This is what one soldier reported: 'We had the pleasure of a grand visitor at the Glen. His Majesty King Haakon came on a day's visit. I was happy to have finished all the paintwork. After I took this job, I had asked over and over again to get some paint and other necessary things to renovate the house and surroundings. Things looked miserable inside and out. Not to mention the boys' rooms. But when I talked to Captain Lassen about this, it was only excuses about money, - mostly bullshit, so I gave up talking to him and went to Major Godfrey. Just a few days later everybody was at full work. All the boys worked eagerly, and you won't believe how nice it became. The King inspected everything, kitchen, dining room, sitting room, the boys' rooms, and he found everything in order, and he thanked us for a good job.

Because of the King's visit we had arranged a sabotage practice. The object was a railway station. The King was very interested. We had arranged for him to sit in a chair where he could see both the object and the runaway-route if the saboteur was detected. The saboteur was indeed detected and fled towards a dam, or small lake down the slope. The King didn't sit for long. When the saboteur ran, the King jumped up and ran with him, while rifle shots flew around their legs from the soldiers who took part in the exercise. The saboteur jumped into the lake and swam, while the King stopped on the shore watching him. Suddenly there was an explosion. The shore was undermined, and the runaway had touched a wire that was stretched across the lake. Turf and moss and water flew up, and the King was neither dry nor clean when things calmed down. He came running up the slope, laughed, and said Oh, it was so realistsic!

A great day for all of us. A few days later we had a letter from our dear Colonel Wilson in London. The King had told him about the experience, and said it had been great fun. He also told us not to lose courage, although it was much waiting.' "

"By 1942, Allied High Command was seriously worried by the possibility of Germany producing atomic weapons. The Norwegian town of Rjukan stands at the foot of the Hardangervidda, and takes its name from the 104 metre waterfall, the 'Rjukan Fossen' which today is a major tourist attraction. This plentiful supply of water is what led Norsk Hydro to open a plant there, to produce electricity. By 1934 they had built what was then the world's largest plant at Vemork. One of the by-products of producing hydro-electricity is 'heavy water', water enriched by the hydrogen isotope deuterium; this is a component of atomic weapons.

Because of this, High Command commited much thought and planning to the destruction of this plant, after it had fallen into Nazi hands. The plans included building a full-scale model of the plant at Brickendonbury House in Hertfordshire, which Churchill's SOE had converted into a training centre for agents and resistance workers in industrial sabotage. One of our Kompani Linge men was sent there: Sergeant Frederik Kayser."

"Yes", said the other, "they dared not use local resistance groups because they were too closely watched; and they ruled out night bombing because of the people who lived nearby. Nor could we use the Catalinas which our pilots flew from Newport-on-Tay, Rjukan was too close to high mountains, and they could not land on frozen lakes."

"Then 2/Lt Joachim Rønneberg was sent to London, with Major Lief Tronstad, to plan the operations. Firstly, four of our Kompani Linge men were born in Rjukan, or very close to it, so it was decided to drop them by parachute on to the Hardangervidda, to gather information and to act as liason: 2/Lts Jens Anton Poulssen and Knut Haugland, and sergeants Arne Kjelstrup and Claus Helberg; that was called, 'Operation Grouse', though once there, they changed their code-name to 'Swallow'."

"Then, on 19 November 1942 the British attempted an attack using gliders, 'Operation Freshman'."

"That was a disaster', said the other, "40 killed, 2 Horsa Gliders and a Halifax bomber lost, and, worse than that, it alerted the Germans, and made our job much harder."

"Nevertheless, Rønneberg was given the go-ahead to proceed with Operation Gunnerside in February 1943. He had first wanted to join the Navy, when he sailed from Norway to Shetland: 'Having been the only one on board with no feeling of seasickness, I was determined to join the Navy as the quickest possible way to active service. After having met Captain Martin Linge for a short interview, followed by an invitation to lunch, I forgot my intention to join the Navy'"

"Now he was asked to take over Linge's job, and to select suitable commandos to go with him to attack the plant at Vemork. Not only that, but he was asked to organise the equipment: 'sleeping bags specially made on advice at a bedding firm's factory in London, ski-boots from Rob Lawrie & Co in Newark, makers of footwear for climbing and Arctic expeditions, whose address was given me by a climber I once met in Scotland, and a variety of winter equipment collected and specially made after a private visit to the Norwegian Army depot in Dumfries.'"

"The men he selected were 2 Lts Knut Haukelid and Kasper Idland, plus sergeants Frederik Kayser, Birger Strømsheim, and Hans Storhaug."

The other man smiled, "Storhaug might have been known for fun as 'the chicken', but we all knew what an outstanding skier he was."

"Well, Gentlemen", I said, "That certainly is a brave story. These young men who ate and slept at this Youth Hostel before I was born, and who trained in these Cairngorm Mountains, they went back to their homeland to fight the invader and became forever famous."

"They were certainly young", replied the commando, "Birger was the oldest, he was 31 at the time."

"And they needed their training and equipment", said the other, "Joachim remebered that they were dropped 18 miles away from their objective, and that it was -20C in those mountains."

"But they certainly succeeded in their duty. The plant at Vemork was so heavily damaged that the German High Command took the decision to withdraw from the scheme."

The other laughed. "Yes, and they thought they would take their heavy water with them, but they ran into Knut Haukelid again, and he helped to sink the ferry that was carrying it."

"Did they return?", I asked. "No, their adventure was only beginning. The Swedish border offered the greatest safety, but they could not go the direct route, that lay through Oslo; so they trekked and skied for something like 250 miles over the high mountains, as much a feat of navigation as anything, and endured much cold and hardship."

"Yes, Frederik and Birger returned to the isolated places of northern Norway and offered shelter for those on the run. Kasper formed a resistance group in Sweden and stayed with it. Joachim took part in further sabotage, blowing up railway lines and bridges. Sergeant Arne Kjelstrup from the Swallow group joined up with Knut Haukelid, and attacked targets when they could. All of them, of course, received the highest military honours of their country, and rightly so."

"Joachim Rønneberg became a journalist. He presented a paper, 'Linge Company and the British' to the joint Norwegian-British Conference in 1962; and he returned to his old haunts here in 1997, at the age of 77, before attending a conference in Glasgow."

We moved into the kitchen and sat down around the large table, relaxed. The first Norwegian smiled at me. "So, perhaps you can now tell us, these huts which we stayed in, which were knocked down for this memorial stone, what happened to them after we left to go back home? Was there still any military connection? They were built in an 'H' shape, Kompani Linge's log book has detailed plans of them."

"You possess Kompani Linge's log book?" I asked. "Oh yes, it survived, but it is now beyond price." He smiled again, and handed me a sheet of paper. "But we have translated this for you" I read it out: "Complement: Company strength, 275; Special Service, 5; Shetland, 56; Reverted, 160; POW's, 7; Killed in action, 57. Commandants STS26: Maj CS Hamilton HLI, Nov 1941; Maj

Godfrey, Sep 1943; Maj Derek Hilton, Jan 1944. Kompani Linge, Company Commanders: Capt Martin Linge, Sep 1940; Maj Helle, Jan 1942; Capt Reidar Kvinge, Apr 1942; Capt Harald Sandvik, Sep 1943."

"Thank you so much for this", I said. "You are welcome, my friend. Now, what became of our huts?"

"Well" I said, "The Royal Marines took over at first, and continued with mountain training. One of their instructors was Tom Patey, who became a famous rock-climber. And I know that they wanted to continue the military connection; the huts were replaced by 'The Norwegian Lodge', a British Army building just a mile up the road towards Ryvoan."

"But peace returned slowly, and by 1960 the area was 'Glenmore National Forest Park'. Their guide book offered this description: 'At Glenmore, the Norwegian Huts are reserved for Youth Organisations, including schools, colleges and universities. These huts consist of one building, comprising two large huts with a communicating apartment. One hut is partitioned into four rooms, used as sleeping quarters. There are no bunks in the sleeping quarters. The other hut is divided into three; cookhouse, office or store, and dining room-cum-common room. The communicating apartment contains sprays, wash hand basins and lavatories. There is a drying room and a hot water system, but fuel, cooking utensils, beds and bedding are not provided. About forty can be accommodated in the huts.'

Their charges were: £8 for 4 weeks, £5 for 2 weeks, £2:10s for 1 week, and £2 for a week-end; applications were to be made to the Conservator of Forests for North Scotland, at 60 Church Street, Inverness.

I am afraid my list of who stayed there is not complete, but these are the ones I know of: Cambridge University, Elgin Academy, Elgin High School, the Steiner School in Edinburgh, the Bishop

Greer High School, and St James Secondary School, Gorton, Manchester.

Shelagh Hewitt kindly wrote this for me: 'The huts, the old Norwegian Hostel, is the building we stayed in every year from 1953. Even now I can picture it inside in great detail. Where else could a group of Manchester schoolchildren stay and have so much fun and freedom? We all loved them. The new ones up on the road to the Green Loch had much better facilities, but they lacked the atmosphere of the Huts. In the early days we came by lorry, stopping over at Loch Lomond Youth Hostel, then we came by train and then the local coal merchant would meet us and ferry us up to the Huts. It wasn't until the new ski road was put up that the journey became less bumpy. Finally we arrived in style by coach! We always came at Whit Week, never missed, unless someone got in first, then we would come in August.'

"Shelagh was there at the time of the big fire at the Sluggan. She remembers that the Head Forester was Mr Robertson, and that his deputy was Mr Frazier. Her most abiding memory of that fire was, 'that we girls spent hours helping the Chief Forester's wife and other ladies make hundreds of sandwiches and gallons of tea to send out to the fire-fighting crews.'

One of Shelagh's ex pupils, Mr J Parry, also wrote this for her: '1952 was the year I remember most, because that year the Reindeer had become acclimatised to Scotland's lichen, and the Osprey had returned to Loch Garten. 1953 was Coronation Year, and we went up to see the reindeer herder's wigwam, it was just like a North American Indian's tent. There were deer skins drying out in the sun, moccasins inside, snow shoes and all types of clothing required for living outdoors. The food was good and plentiful and we all drank from mountain streams which were pure and cold to the taste. Back in the Huts, the lads' sleeping mattresses were palliases, sacks filled with straw, blankets for covers, and we all slept around a wood burning stove, that kept the main common room very warm during the night. The teachers slept on camp beds, and the girls that came with us had their own room and camp beds too. The lights went out every night at ten o'clock, when the generator was shut down. After that, we depended on Tilly lamps during the night.'

"We thank you very much for that", said the Norwegians, "so may we now eat, and await your other guests?"
"If I may detain you just a little longer," I said, "I wish to tell you my own story of my encounter with something you left behind." Their eyes widened.

"It was one of those idyllic days which only the month of May can produce; incredibly light shades of green all around, an all-pervading sense of freshness in the air, and sunshine seeping everywhere. My uncle and aunt had gone on holiday, and we had about 30 people staying in the hostel, including a group of eight Portuguese girls. In the late afternoon I was wending my way back after a hard day on the beach, when I was met by my friend Rob, who, with a touch of anxiety and excitement in his voice, said: 'You had better come and look at what we have found.' We walked around the back of the Hostel and there, lying on the path, was what looked to all intents and purposes like a hand grenade! 'The dogs found it up there', said Rob, waving his hand towards the forest a little way up the hill, 'carried it to here, and dropped it. What do you make of it?'

What did we make of it? Some kind of toy crossed my mind, and yet it was obviously made of metal. Two things were immediately apparent: there were red 'Xs' painted on it, and the top of it was open, no 'pin'. We reasoned it out. some kind of toy dating from the 50's or 60's seemed unlikely. A hand grenade from the war without a pin was surely impossible.

'We ought not to leave it lying on the path', said Rob. At the other end of the building the telephone people had built a concrete slab to park their vans; to one side of it, there was a small ditch. I picked the thing up and carried it, very cautiously, perhaps for 40 or 50 yards and placed it, very carefully, in the ditch. We felt better, not totally convinced, but better; our part was done. We opened the Hostel and booked in three or four people.

Still, we could not settle, and we discussed further what it could possibly be. By far the best solution, as we saw it, was to let the Police have a look at it, they could sort it out, and we could return to normality. I telephoned Aviemore Police. 'Could you please describe in a bit more detail what you have found?' I described it. 'Good Heavens, please put the phone down, someone will get back to you.'

That did not settle us down very much at all. The phone rang. 'Good evening, this is Rothiemurchus Lodge, Army here; could you please describe what you have found?' I described it. 'Goodness Gracious, please now put the phone down, someone will get back to you.' 'No please wait', I said, 'we are really not sure it might be just a toy. All we want is someone to come and look at it.' 'It is not a toy, someone will call you soon.'

I went outside and looked at the mountains, serene and majestic in the evening sunshine. My hands were shaking. The phone rang. 'This is RAF Lossiemouth here, can you please describe what you have found?' I told them about the red Xs and that it had no pin as far as I could see.

'Good Heavens, where is it now?' I told them I had put it in a small ditch, for safety. 'You carried it?' he sounded incredulous, 'Is it near to the building?' 'Ok, Thank you. We will arange things, please put the phone down; someone will contact you.' 'Good Luck', he added.

I wished I was somewhere else. We walked back to the 'thing' and looked at it again, from a very safe distance. For the first time, I shivered and felt a little afraid.

The phone rang. 'Good evening', said a classic officer's voice, 'This is Army Bomb Disposal, Edinburgh here. Please can you tell me exactly where the grenade is?' I tried hard to speak. 'Look I am really not sure it is a grenade, you know. All we want is for someone to come and look at it.' 'Never mind that; is it close to the building? A Youth Hostel, I believe?'
'Er, Yes, and we have about 30 guests.' 'Right-O. Please clear everyone out of that side of the building. We will contact Aviemore Police to send someone to guard it, and we will be right up.'
Right up? Did he say right up? from Edinburgh? We were nervous wrecks. We could see the Strathy headlines: 'Edinburgh Army Bomb Disposal called out to Loch Morlich Youth Hostel for a child's toy'.

I cannot claim to speak Portuguese fluently, certainly not with adequate vocabulary to cover, 'Please get up, there is a second world war hand grenade about to go off outside your window'. We found a kind lady, who said that her Portuguese wasn't that good either, but she would do her best.

A nice Police lady arrived, and was astonishingly matter-of-fact about it all. 'What a lovely evening. Have you got everybody out? All I shall need is a chair, please.' The hostellers had collectively decided that the best idea was a walk on the beach, for which I was immensely grateful. We made coffee and sandwiches; a deep feeling came over me that it was all out of our hands now, anyway.

Dusk fell, and I watched two Army landrovers trundle up the hostel drive, one with a trailer. Several soldiers got out, and a tall Lieutenant introduced himself with an immensely re-assuring smile, and a hand shake which hurt my fingers. 'Well, lets have a look at your grenade, then.' He marched with military precision in his step up to the small ditch by the telephone exchange. What followed was a moment which will stay with me for the rest of my life. The Lieutenant looked into the ditch, and instinctively recoiled with a look of some horror. He issued rapid orders to his men. 'Sand-bag it. We'll have to detonate it where it is. Not safe to move.'

Did he say 'not safe to move?' I cannot adequately describe my feelings.

The Lieutenant turned to me; 'Have you got everybody out of the building?' 'All clear?' 'Good.'

Soldiers scurried around, the ditch was filled with sand bags, and, using a pair of extending tongs, they very, very carefully attached wires to our 'thing'. They rolled the wires all the way back down the path and round behind the building. The sergeant was there, with a box with two red buttons on it; they attached the wires to the box. Soldiers were dispatched everywhere, to check that all was in good order.

'You press those two red buttons, together', smiled the Lieutenant. I remember being disappointed that it wasn't a plunger! We decided that we really ought to let the nice Police lady do the deed.

The blast shattered two of the windows where the girls had been; but what I remember most is that the shock wave rolled across the glen, re-bounded off the northern corries, and rattled all the windows in the front of the Hostel.

Back in the safety of this kitchen, we offered strong coffee and good malt whisky. The Lieutenant opted for coffee; we and the Police lady chose the whisky. The Lieutenant slowly raised his eyes. 'Tell me', he said, 'is there by any chance any connection with Norwegians here?' We told him. 'To some extent, that explains about the pin,' he said. 'They developed the idea of throwing the grenade with a roll of paper tied to the pin; the paper, snapping taut, would pull out the pin in mid air and thus cause more damage. Norwegian idea.'

'Of course, why this one didn't explode is still a mystery; but they nearly got you, didn't they? And your generation would not know it, but every kid in their time would have known that red Xs meant TNT; there was rather a lot of it in your grenade.' He rose to leave, and thanked us. 'And you,' he said warmly, 'are two very lucky lads.' And so we are."

The Forester's Tale

A knock, and the kitchen door opened. In walked a man, so tall he had to duck to enter. Deerstalker hat, knee breeches, boots and a green jacket with a badge bearing the words, 'Glenmore National Forest Park'. He held out his right hand; in his left he carried a bottle of good malt whisky. He shook my hand. "Thank you for your kind invitation. I have brought this so we can all enjoy a wee dram as I tell my story." He opened the bottle. "Cheers, and here's to a good, wet Easter." (A traditional forester's greeting.) We sat down, and he began his tale.

"We were there from the beginning, you know. The original lodge built by their Lordships, that burnt down in 1870, but this one, well, we purchased it in 1923." He pulled a paper from one of his many pockets, and read out loud: "The Forestry Commission purchased the Glenmore Lodge with effect from Martinmas, 1923, as part of the Disposition by the Most Noble Charles Henry Gordon Lennox, Duke of Richmond Gordon and Lennox KG, and the Right Honourable Charles Henry Gordon Lennox, Earl of March and Darnley, in favour of the Forestry Commission, 9 and 12 November 1923."

He smiled, "We had to be involved. The original, ancient Scots Pine was first much reduced by grazing in the 17th century; but the two World Wars caused absolute devastation; Canadian foresters felled most of it during the Second World War, as I am sure you Gentlemen will know." He nodded towards the Norwegians.

"We had two major periods of re-afforestation: 2,100 acres between 1924 and 1933, and 1,100 acres from 1949 to 1960. Scots Pine, Lodgepole Pine and Sitka Spruce is what we planted. The large patch of fenced forest still visible today up by Coire na Ciste was an experiment to see what might grow above the natural tree line."

"We established the 'Queen's Forest of Glenmore' in 1948, and so it was marked on the OS maps. That was named after the Silver Jubilee of King George V and Queen Mary. Argyll became the first National Forest Park, and we became the second. In 1953, to mark the Coronation, the 'Queen Elizabeth National Forest Park' was created by the side of Loch Lomond."

He turned to address the commandos. "They continued with military training for about two years after you left. The Royal Marines took charge of the huts, and the Coldstream Guards used the campsite and the beach for winter exercises. But slowly, peace returned to Glenmore, and the Lodge reverted to the Forestry Commission. We recognised a need for the young generation, and so we were prepared to lease it out to groups and organisations with an interest in the hills and in physical recreation."

"Then, just before Easter 1947, a one-week course was held based at the Aviemore Hotel. What a course that was, you might say that the great and the good were there. It was led by Lord Malcolm, instructors included Lady David Douglas Hamilton, Mr "Jock" Kerr Hunter, Dr N.E.Odell (a member of the 1924 and 1938 Everest expeditions), Mr Charles Cromar, and Major Alastair Erskine Murray, who was known on all subsequent courses as "Dougie". Hugh Ross, in charge of the Hotel, made sure that all were looked after and fed. Not surprisingly, this led to the establishment of Glenmore Lodge, and on 14 November 1947 we leased the building to them for a period of ten years. The Rev RJV (Bob) Clark was the first warden, and Robin Murray was in charge of field pursuits. May Brown became the Secretary, and was a good driving force behind the encouragement of outdoor pursuits."

"Do not forget", I said, "that the road from Coylumbridge then was no more than a rough vehicle track, only really suitable for lorries, and that, from the Lodge, everyone had to trudge up the Allt

Mor carrying skis or mountaineering equipment, and the only shelter was at the Clach Bharraig Bothy."

"Ah", replied the Forester, "The ski road; that is another story for another time." He turned again to the Norwegians. "And, talking of the great and the good, your huts", he said, " will be forever famous as the first meeting-place between two legends: Frith Finlayson and Jack Thomson, at New Year 1951-2 where the Creah Dhu Climbing Club were gathered."

"Well", I said, "the history of Glenmore Lodge itself has certainly been well documented. In 1952 Catharine Loader published: 'Cairngorm Adventure at Glenmore Lodge', and in 2003, 'A History of Glenmore Lodge' by the venerable IDS Thomson was published as an e-book by the Scottish Mountaineering Trust.

I find it interesting that Catharine Loader, in her introduction, said that it was neither a guide book nor a textbook, but that, "We want the young people to come to Glenmore to explore unfrequented ways and to discover the secrets of the forest paths; once discovered, they become a never-ending source of delight, a key to adventure in a new world, and possibly to a happier way of life." And that Murray Scott, writing his introduction for IDS Thomson, picked up the same theme: he talked about bringing youngsters from the cities to places such as Glenmore, and what he called, "The alchemy of forest, loch and mountain will do the rest." He also described Glenmore as, "a self-contained community, virtually cut off from the outside world." In many ways," I said, "It still is."
The tall forester relaxed, poured himself another dram, and before he sat down, pulled some more papers from his pockets.

"Discussions", he announced "between the three of us, Forestry, Glenmore Lodge, SYHA began as early as 1955." I expressed some surprise at this; "I have the minutes here", said the forester. "There can be no doubt, ski-ing was becoming ever more popular throughout the 50's, and 60's for that matter. So Glenmore Lodge needed an extension, and something had to be done about standards of instructing. It was the Lodge who decided it was more economical to move to a new building than to extend the present one, so they consulted us, Forestry Commission, and asked Murray Scott to identify suitable new sites. They also had one eye on the lease that we granted them, which was due to expire in 1957. Eventually they decided to move to the Allt Ban site where, the present Glenmore Lodge still stands. The Scottish Education Department agreed, and the new Glenmore Lodge opened in May 1959."

"And what about ski teaching?" I prompted. He turned once again to the Norwegians seated around the table, and laughed. "You gentlemen and your countrymen will certainly never be forgotten, whatever happens." He read again from his paper. "In 1955 the three interested parties decided to hold a training course for Instructors at Garth Youth Hostel. I quote: 'We invited the Norwegian School of Skiing to send an outstanding instructor to act as tutor. It was felt that Norwegian skiing conditions are nearer to those experienced in Scotland than those of most other European countries, and that it would be wise to learn from our Norwegian friends, many of whom skied in the Cairngorms during the war years.'"

The Forester turned to me. "Glenmore 'grew up' as things were slowly improving during the 1950's. Rationing eventually came to an end, and the National Grid arrived to provide electricity in 1959, just before SYHA took over the building. The stone buildings just over the little bridge were originally stables for the shooting lodge, but the nearest one became Glenmore Church for a while. Freddie Salter was the Minister, and there were times during the summer months when you had to arrive early for his Sunday evening service, or you would have to stand outside. Just behind that, the

31

red stone house was for the gamekeeper; and we built two grey stone houses, for Head Forester and Assistant Forester.

Head Foresters were Jackie Fraser, followed by David Robertson, who was in that post when Glenmore Lodge became Loch Morlich Hostel; then Alastair Morison, Alastair McCleod, Willie Grant and Rodney McCleod. Tony Hinde was one of the Assistant Foresters. Alastair Morison became Head Forester of the Queen's Forest in 1971, and retired from the post in 1979 to Nethybridge. Of course he was responsible for the upkeep of the forest and all that entails, but he also took the bookings for the campsite and the Norwegian Huts."

"Yes," I replied, "Mr Morison was always very kind to me. I remember him coming into the Hostel and sharing a dram with my uncle and giving the same toast you just gave us! I also came to know his children well, Kathleen, and Alan who worked for a short time at the Hostel from 1973-74. The other stone house in Glenmore was for the reindeer keeper, then?" I asked him. "Oh Yes, we did not build that one. Mikel Utsi was approached, about testing them in a new region as early as 1947, but the reindeer themselves came over between 1952 and 1955, by iron-ore boat, lorry and train. All of which was organised by the Reindeer Council of the UK." "Really?", I asked. "Which was chaired", he went on, "by Sir Frederick Whyte, KCSI, no less; and before you ask, that stands for 'Knight Commander of the Star of India'! By the time the Youth Hostel opened, 15 of those reindeer were Scottish born; we have much to thank Mikel Utsi for, and his wife, Dr Lűndgren."

"Because of its setting and spectacular views, we also were obliged to develop the camping site after the soldiers had left it. It was simply a flat field, no paths around it, nor a road leading to it; nevertheless we knew many people would come to stay. We already employed some foresters, so we allocated some to be campsite wardens. Not only that, but between 1950 and 1955 we used wood from Paddy's Field and built four houses for them. The first warden was Louis Robertson, after him Aeneas Cameron, then Alastair Dow, then Jimmy Docherty, then Alan McDougall.

Prior to that, they had stayed in the green-painted Forestry Commission Hostel at the side of the building. Everyone there would have known of Dolly and Bunty, who cleaned and polished everything, helped with all the meals, and who have achieved deserved and lasting fame in IDS Thomson's book. The wardens, though, were Jimmy and Annie Reid, who came originally from the Aberdeen area. Mrs Reid it was who became chief cook, and her meals quickly became legendary."

The tall Forester turned towards me, his face becoming serious. "And that is why," he said, "although we leased the building to SYHA, and re-negotiated that lease in November 1977 and again in March 1985, written into the terms and conditions of the original lease in 1960, we stipulated that Mrs Reid, (after her husband died) shoud have free accommodation in the Hostel for the rest of her life." "We were happy to honour that" I replied. "At the far side of the common room there was a door, and then another door into her flat, and indeed there she stayed for the rest of her life."

The District Secretary, his Tale

A knock at the kitchen door, this time, and outside stood two smartly dressed gentlemen, sports jackets and trousers, smart black shoes. I ushered them into the hostel's large, warm, friendly catering kitchen, and they each shook me warmly by the hand. I introduced them to the others. "May I present, the District Secretary of the Dundee Branch, SYHA, and his Clerk of Works." "Well, that certainly has the looking of a goodly feast to which you have so kindly invited us", said the Secretary, "but, as your invitation states, first we must tell our story. I wonder, may we come with you into the rest of the building?"

They followed me out of the kitchen, into the 'washing-up kitchen', and turned right along the small corridor leading to the hall. They stopped at the first room on the left. "Ah' said the Clerk of Works, "this is now the Quiet Room, but for a good while at first it was the Warden's Office. A counter running down the middle of the room, towards the window, with a hatch; and behind the counter was the office store room. This is where the first wardens, including your Uncle, used to book people in, and of course sell them milk, chocolate bars, SYHA badges, and postcards."

We wandered into the hall and stood in front of the Warden's Office. "For much of it's time" said the Clerk, "this was the Baggage Room; with dormitory accommodation, space was always limited, so this room served a useful purpose."

We opened the door into the Common Room. "Then as now" said the Clerk, "it has always been a Common Room, hard-wearing asphalt floor, plenty of large tables, and lots of chairs. People could gather, play board games, have sing-songs, and even talk to each other! At least they did before that machine was put in." he said, gesturing towards the TV set. "But you see the door at the far end.

Through that you went into the flat which we made up for Mrs Reid, as agreed with Glenmore Lodge. It had a Yale lock."

"It remained as a flat for a little while after that good lady died" I said, "I remember that Harry Jamieson, one of our first instructors, came back from Switzerland with his wife, Christianne, and until they could find a house, they too stayed in the flat."

We returned to the hall, and pulled open the heavy door into the front porch. On the right was a small, arched alcove with two wooden shelves. "The Boot Room" announced the Clerk of Works, "and dead ahead was the old front door, opening straight out onto the garden." "A double door it was, white on the outside, blue painted wooden panels on the inside. Many a time I locked it, top and bottom bolts, and at 10:45!" I said. "Do you know, so my Uncle told me, at the end of one summer we counted 28 pairs of walking boots which were left and nobody had bothered to claim them." "Ah" said the District Secretary, wistfully, "if SYHA had gathered all the un-claimed boots and all the towels that were left in hostels and sold them in the market place, well, we would have a bit more money than we do now, shall we say."

We returned to the hall and there I stopped both gentlemen. "It was precisely at his point," I said "that many people will remember my uncle greeting them with a single word, which was delivered in what I can best describe as a Stentorian voice: 'BOOTS'. I also think" I added, "that every single person who received that greeting will remember him with affection."

The Clerk of Works led us past the Warden's Office door, and turned left down the long tiled corridor, into what was the old wooden section of the building. "This first door on the right" he said, "was the Members' Kitchen."

"How warm that room always was" I said, "and how busy it was for most of the year. That was why my Uncle had another phrase for which he was well known: 'I only have two sorts of pans in this kitchen; clean ones and full ones!'"

"Tayco stoves were in this kitchen and in the catering kitchen, inherited from Glenmore Lodge" explained the Clerk of Works. "Square things, about a metre high, coke or any solid fuel, large black flues leading into the walls, their prime fuction was to heat the water. They had a stoking hole at the top, and a removeable ash tray at the bottom; you could turn them down at night so that they would be still alight in the morning."

"Sometimes they were not" I replied, "and sometimes that would affect my Uncle's mood for quite a while! But once again, many hostellers remembered that old kitchen, with its tables and wooden benches, and its cubby holes with great affection."   "It was in November 1977 that we made the alterations to it." said the Clerk.

"Next, on this side was a much smaller room, and the door was labelled: 'Chief Instructor'." "As far as my memory serves me" I replied, "the first occupant of that room was Robin Stephens, and the last person to use that room as Chief Instructor was big Ron McLelland. I remember it was also used for a season by Alex Snaddon; he was a great hero of mine, and I was devastated when I heard he had been killed in a ski-ing accident in New Zealand."

"Then, at the bottom of the corridor on the left was a huge room which could sleep four, five or six instructors" said the Clerk. "It had two large windows which looked out straight down the Hostel drive and towards Loch Morlich; those windows were sometimes used for, shall I say, 'out-of-hours' access! Perhaps Alex Ferguson, Rab Smith and Billy McLean could testify about that! It is also where I stayed during my first two long, idyllic summer holidays from school" I said.

"Then on to the right, down a short dark passageway, were two old, cold and damp dorms, the dreaded 'J' and 'K' dorms." I shivered; "I remember sleeping there, with the wind whistling through the gaps in the wooden walls, I used to put more clothes on to go to bed, instead of taking them off. The main mens' washrooms were there also; it was at a time when I was realising that I had to shave every day, and I did not like icicles hanging from my chin!"

"Between the rooms was a cupboard where my uncle used to store all his tools. He always enjoyed doing odd jobs, especially wood-working," I said. "We certainly appreciated that," said the Clerk "every Youth Hostel stands in need of someone who can do that, but it was between 1973 and 1977 that we made the major alterations to the building which transformed it into mostly how it appears today. We were in consultation with the Forestry Commission all the while, and we decided to split the work into two stages. We really had to bring it up to the best standard possible, because it was during those years that ski-ing was becoming ever more popular, in fact your Hostel was in the process of becoming the SYHA' s premier sports hostel. At the same time, of course, we cut down the number of beds, gradually making it more comfortable."

"Yes," I replied, "we could sleep about 126 at first; that was cut to 72 in 1977, and then gradually increased to about 86. Our peak year for ski bookings was 1984, we had to use a double-decker bus!"

"Most of the accommodation was upstairs, of course" said the Clerk. "Moving anti-clockwise from the top of the stairs, there were six dormitories, A,B,C,D,E and F." We walked around them, passing through the door of the partitioning wall by 'C' dorm.
"We carried on a tradition from old Glenmore Lodge days," I said "we called them 'Angels Peak', 'Braeriach', 'Cairngorm', 'Devils Point', 'Einich', and 'Fiacaill'. The dorms at the front all had stunning views of the mountains."

The Clerk of Works turned, and walked past the top of the stairs, into the Wardens' flat, which the Norwegains had used as the radio room. "We were working to get the place ready for opening in 1961." he said, "We lifted the floorboards in what became the sitting room, the one with the fire escape outside, and we found a bullet from a 45 revolver embedded in one of the joists. Now that might have come from the old shooting lodge days, or your Norwegain friends downstairs might have been responsible. It was Bob Duncan who took it and kept it as a souvenir, but we do not know what happened to it after that!"

"There was, of course, a balcony outside this room, with a fire escape which was for many years a feature of the outside of the hostel frontage."

We returned down the stairs and greeted the guests back in the kitchen; but the Clerk of Works insisted on taking us into the room behind the kitchen. "This is where I shall complete my story" he said. "Two large rooms were here, and in the corner, in the turret, was a bathroom. During the first alterations we split the outer room into two, for the kitchen assistants. The room we are standing in was the staff sitting room."

"Ah," I said "I can remember this with affection. Many, many great stories have been told and re-told in this room; every member of staff has passed in and out of here. For many years its most remarkable feature was its music. I never knew how they managed it, but my Uncle and Auntie brought their pianola with them from Chadderton. Two great wooden pedals at the bottom, which we pressed with gusto; two boxes full of rolls of music; the room echoed to the merry sounds of 'The Poet and the Peasant', 'Echoes from the Pantomimes', 'The Trumpeter', 'The Cornish Floral Dance', and 'Glorious Devon'.

Many a hosteller whose duty it was to help peel the potatoes, or to do the washing up would have heard the distant strains of that music. Perhaps they thought that we had some quite talented pianists among the staff!"

The Clerk and I seated ourselves in the comfortable chairs around the low coffee table. The District Secretary remained standing, and he thoughtfully began his tale.

"Mine is a story far more concerned with people, rather than buildings." He smiled. "But I can begin it right here in this very room. This, when it was all one large room, was where Mrs Bull used to serve the Hostel meals."

"The wife of Captain, or Major Bull?" we questioned. "Quite so," replied the Secretary, "and I am not quite certain of his rank either, but I am already getting a little ahead of myself."

"When we first opened the doors as a Youth Hostel in 1960, we had not appointed permanent wardens. The Aviemore staff helped out, Derek Young came for a short while, and so did Alasdair, whom we might describe nowadays as 'partially sighted'. Then Stuart and Molly, the wardens at Strathtummel agreed to take over until we could appoint full time wardens. That is when the Captain (or Major) Bull and his good lady took over the running of the hostel."

"The accounts and memories that we have of these two are these: 'He was just retired from the Army; not sure of his rank, but he certainly behaved as a Sergeant-Major, barking orders before we even got through the entrance door.' and, 'She, not posh by any means, but better dressed and better made up than most.'"

"It is imortant to remember that all of this would have been overseen by 'JL', or Jim Taylor and his wife Cathie. Jim contributed 50 years of his life to the SYHA and rose to become Honorary Vice President, but in the early days, he and his wife were stalwarts of the work parties which were so much a part of that era."

"Yes, indeed," replied the Clerk of Works, "the cost of restoring and renovating such an old and vast building would have been far too high for us to contemplate, and we owe a tremendous debt to the volunteer work parties who made it all possible. The local newspaper, 'The Strathy', was certainly impressed."

"On 8 April 1960 it had this to say: 'The old Glenmore Lodge has been renamed as Loch Morlich Youth Hostel and is undergoing internal alterations. The work is being done at week-ends by voluntary work parties from Dundee, Inverness and Fort William. After Easter, it will be closed, so that the volunteers will really be able to get down to it. Bedrooms are being converted to Dormitories, it will sleep 100. There are rubber floor coverings, contemporary wallpaper and pastel shades of paint. The water in the building will be heated by liquid gas and operated by coin-in-the-slot.'"

"So, then, the Hostel was open while this work was being carried out?" I questioned. "Oh Yes, replied the Clerk, as the 'Strathy' itself reported: 'A Party of students from Bristol University are at present on a course at Loch Morlich, receiving ski-ing tuition from expert instructors.' Your ski teaching predecessors go back further than you thought. But the 'Strathy' was even more impressed a year later, especially by the contemporary decoration; this is from 17 March, 1961: 'When the Duke of Edinburgh visits Loch Morlich on Thursday 23 March, he will see there one of the most modern of Youth Hostels, which is becoming more and more popular, as it makes it possible for more young people to walk, climb and ski in the Cairngorms. It has been possible for the SYHA to do this work only because of the tremendous enthusiasm and devotion of its volunteer work parties from Dundee. Without them the cost would have been prohibitive. The work parties travelled by lorry over 100 miles each way at week-ends, while two members gave up their summer holidays to rid the spider-infested lofts of the woodworm beatle! The result is a modern hostel up to the highest continental standards, with 90 beds, heated dorms and hot showers. It is surprising to find contemporary decor in a remote building, but this building, which is now in the service of youth, has been rejuvenated and its bright colours are symbolic of the fresh and original outlook of youth itself.'"

The District Secretary smiled again. "I suggest that might be a fitting, though hardly adequate testimony to dear Jim and Cathie Taylor." he said.

"Another who was around at that time was of course Jack Frame, who went on to become Vice President of SYHA. Jack it was who wrote the article for the 'Scottish Hosteller' magazine in January 1960. He began his article thus: 'The new Loch Morlich Hostel will be available for use on 23 January. An official opening is planned for May.' He waxed lyrical about the opportunities which would be offered to the young people by providing, 'beds, available at a price anyone can afford.' and he finished by saying that, 'at last we will have a hostel within easy reach of the Cairngorms; ski-ing, mountaineering and field studies - all these are now possible.'"

"Then there were the Cromar brothers, Charles and Arthur. Each was well known amongst the foremost 'mountain men' of their day, formidable climbers and skiers, but each dedicated his time to the service of youth. Charles P Cromar was on the CCPR staff in Glasgow, and his work included introducing physical recreation to school leavers. He became warden of Glenmore Lodge, and his wife was Secretary and Housekeeper; for a while she ran a little sweet shop at the Lodge.

Arthur was for many years General Secretary of SYHA, retiring in 1968.

He learnt much of his mountain-craft in the Alps, but on making the acquaintance of Eilif Moen, he began travelling in Norway, staying at the Norwegian Youth Hostels, developing affection for them, and learning about the way they were administered. This knowledge he passed on to SYHA.

The letters after his name were MA and LLD, which means he was a Master of Arts and a Bachelor of Law; nevertheless he too dedicated his services to outdoor education, and he wrote articles on canoeing and ski-ing, and, along with the botanist Donald Patton, he produced the SYHA's guide to Garth and Glen Lyon, which work was: 'a labour of love, and the special articles in it have been written by experts with a view to introducing many young people to outdoor sports, ski-ing and climbing, and to new fields of study, of the rich flora and fauna and archaeology.'

That was taken from the foreward to the book. Now," the District Secretary's eyes sparkled "by way of storytelling, you will no doubt be pleased to know that in the summer of 1946, the Edinburgh University Mountaineering Club decided that the ideal venue for an informal dinner should be Ryvoan Bothy; that dinner was characterised by, 'the consumption of copious amounts of food and alcohol, and incomprehensible speeches.' In the autumn, that same august body elected three Honorary Members to their Club. The first two were Gordon Scott and Dr Drever, and the third was, 'Arthur Cromar, Secretary of that excellent and essential organisation, the SYHA.'

The Cromars had a dog, which went with them onto the mountains" added the District Secretary, "he was called Figaro!"

"So please tell us what happened at the official opening" I asked. "There is no doubt" he said, "that SYHA were both pleased and proud to acquire this building as a hostel. The hope was expressed that, 'this may be the first of a group of youth hostels on the perimeter of the great massif of the Cairngorms'. Indeed, Jack Frame finished his article for the SYHA magazine by writing this: '..at last we will have a hostel within easy reach of the Cairngorms....if only the hosteller could cross the plateau and find another SYHA hostel similarly placed on Derry side! Loch Morlich has been long in coming, maybe the time for a Derry hostel will come too.' That explains why we carefully timed our official opening to coincide with a Royal visit to Strathspey."

"The Duke has long been a patron of SYHA, and we are grateful for that. On 23 March 1961, however, he came first to visit the new Glenmore Lodge, and to inspect their new premises. He was then taken on a rather eventful ride up to Coire Cas in the Lodge landrover, with warden and chauffeur Murray Scott.

What he saw 'up the hill' is of some interest: firstly he would have seen 'Jean's Hut' in its original position, just a little to the side of where the White Lady Sheiling stood for so many years. He would also have seen the preparations for building a chairlift from the Sheiling to nearly the top of Cairngorm. His visit was in fact instrumental in raising the money necessary to build that, and the White Lady Chairlift was officially opened, with due ceremony, on 23 December 1961.

He also saw a demonstration of ski-ing by local instructors. Archie Scott, who did much of the organising, realised how little snow there was and organised nine instructors to shovel snow onto the White Lady, actually onto the strip of snow which forms one side of the 'skirt', towards Coire Cas. Eilif Moen had a team of young instructors from Norway with him, and he demonstrated teaching with a class from Grantown Grammar School. Karl Fuchs, George McLeod and Jack Thompson were part of the ski demonstration team, and Karl's 5 year old son, Peter, impressed everybody by a perfect descent of the White Lady in a wide-stance snow-plough! Afterwards, Eilif and the Duke chatted for a while. The Duke asked if there was any more young talent available to Scottish ski teaching. Eilif replied that training centres and courses were being set up; the Duke thought that was "splendid". Alas, our first Chief Instructor, Robin Stephens was not there."

"And then, the Duke came to visit our new Youth Hostel. It was the great and the good who formed a reception committee," the District Secretary smiled, "in fact the Glasgow people had been working hard, travelling around giving slide shows to promote the association and organising social gatherings between the other districts. They were all there to meet the Duke: William Ballantyne, SYHA President and Director of the Bank of Scotland, Bill Nelson, Glasgow district secretary, Anne Gillie and Bob Sawyers, Jimmy Crawford, Andy Bennet, Alister Scott, Ina Campbell and Jimmy Morland.

Dundee were well represented also; Doug Scobie the bricklayer, Bob Duncan the slater and harler, and his wife Norma, and Alex Ferguson the electrician. All of these were presented to the Duke of Edinburgh as he walked through the same door which the King of Norway had entered all those years before.

Once inside, as the 'Strathy' reported, 'The Duke made a twenty minute tour of Loch Morlich Youth Hostel, inspecting the accommodation, and chatting with the staff and the young hostellers; those included 28 pupils of Inverness Royal Academy, and boys from Buckhaven High School.'"

"And so" concluded the District Secretary, "Loch Morlich Hostel officially began its long life in the service of youth, blessed by a Royal visitor. I will conclude my story" he said rather wistfully, "by telling you something which Jack Frame mentioned: 'The old Glenmore Lodge is now a large Youth Hostel named Loch Morlich, after the loch beside which it stands, and to avoid confusion with the new Glenmore Lodge of the SCPR.'!"

The Ski Instructors; their Tale

Four cheerful faces appeared at the window; two young gentlemen and two young ladies, each of them clad in a smart two-tone blue ski suit with a circular badge which proclaimed, 'SYHA Ski School, Loch Morlich'.

"Hello", they chorused, "we have such a long and wonderful tale to tell you. Let us begin it, if we may, in our base of operations. Could you please pass us the Ski Room key?" That prompted immediate laughter from all, "It was always known to us as 'the key room ski.'" Everyone agreed with that.

We linked arms as we walked down the passage-way to the door at the far end. Entering the Ski Room, we all sat down on the bench to our left, and gazed, smiling, down the full length of that room. "It is so very good that we are together again", I said, "You are most welcome here, Billy, Rab, Rosie and Chris." Immediately in front of us was a wooden counter. "We have all of us stood behind that counter many times, mainly to issue equipment to the ski courses on a Saturday night", said Billy. "Poles were on racks to the left; we would turn one upside down, get you to rest your arm on the 'basket', and if your arm was at a right-angle, the pole was the right size for you."

"The ski boots", said Rosie, "functional they certainly were; warm and comfortable they may not have been!" "As far back as I can remember, we even had lace-up leather boots here for a while, and the black rubber ones with four clips served us for many years before we got the posh Salomon plastic one-clip boots. So many people told us that they had different size feet, and so many changed them again after one or two days. But it did not matter, and I think most will remember them with a kind of affection."

"Skis!" announced Chris. She stood up, and raised her right hand above her head. "That how long they used to be," she said, "seems hard to believe in these days of carvers, but it was the ideal length for the skis we had to work with."

"Do you remember which skis were around in the early days?" I asked. She smiled: "There were Hagan skis, if you can remember them. The 'Prima' was made in Austria, all wood, with small metal plates attached to the tip and the tail with rivets; delta-wing badge, painted dark blue. Cable bindings, with Marker toe pieces. Goodness only knows how anyone managed to turn them, but they did! Fischer, Blizzard, Kneissl and Atomic were all Austrian made, and Head came from USA. Cable bindings were the norm for many years, you pulled the cable onto the ridge at the back of your boot, and then leaned right forward to press down the metal lever to lock it! You had to keep your gloves on, mind, because that lever could be very cold. It was the American company, Ess-Nevada, which became Look, which introduced the step-in binding, and the French Salomon took it on from there.

For the years from 1970 to 1984, our market was dominated by an Austrian called Leopold Vielhaber. He experimented with a layered system of building a ski, using fibreglass and Kevlar; this led to names for his skis such as 'Carbon-Flex', 'Black Fusion', and the 'Carbon-Fibre Multi-Torsion Box Fusion System'! He began the British section of his business in Birnham in Perthshire, and was so successful that he built a factory in Aviemore, (where Spey Valley Hire is now.) More importantly, he made his skis tough and durable, ideal for Scottish general conditions.

Our chief instructor, Plum, recognised the value of this, and so for all those years and afterwards, Vielhaber skis were the mainstay of our ski hire, and in truth they lasted remarkably well and needed little maintainance."

"Yes," replied Billy, "I can remember their logo on posters all over the place: 'We make tracks, others follow.' "

We moved slowly out of the ski room, turned to the right, down two stone steps and out into the bright sunshine.

"So on the whole," said Rosie, "I think we did our ski course people proud with the equipment we issued to them."

"As for warm clothing," said Chris, "we left that largely up to themselves."

"It is strange to think," said Billy, "that Lillywhites of Edinburgh began life as a supplier of cricket goods; but they came to play a large part in dressing people for the ski slopes. But of course the largest supplier of skiwear was C & A, with their 'Rodeo' range of jackets and salopettes."

"Yes," replied Rab, "they called it their 'budget' range, but 'cheap and cheerful' was the more usual description, especially during the mid-80's, when the blacks, greys and blues were replaced with a rainbow of colours. It was affordable, warm, almost waterproof, and it made the ski slopes a colourful place to be."

We walked through the back door of the Hostel and made our way towards the common room.

"Affordable!" said Rosie, thoughtfully. "I should like to think that most people would say that our whole ski-course package was good value for money, especially as we kept it not too far above the £100 mark for most of the years."

"I am certain that they would," said Billy, "when you think about everything that package included for the week. It would begin on the Saturday night when a coach would go down to Aviemore railway station to meet the London train. As the years went by, more and more began to arrive in their own cars, but the coach was always there for those who needed it."

"Indeed it was," I said, "and I will always have the utmost respect for those Highland Omnibus drivers. I remember one wild winters night when the train could get no further than Kingussie because of the drifting snow. But our Highland boys managed to get their coach down the road, and they brought everyone back to the warmth and safety of the Hostel."

"Quite so," said Chris, "a hot meal on the Saturday was always provided, until as late as was practical. After which, we would bring folk into the ski room in threes and fours and issue the skis boots and poles. Prior to that we would have sorted out with the Chief Instructor who was taking which class for the week. We all know that we worked on a rota basis, one or two weeks with beginners, then those who had skied a little before, and then the top class. It was just so lovely when people began to return for two or three years."

"Yes," said Rosie, "the list of names which the SYHA sent us week by week began to look like a list of friends."

"I can certainly say how much I appreciated that," I said. "I remember one Easter when our 'rotation' system simply did not work. We had 86 people on the ski course, including the famous 'Rock-Hoppers Ski Club' from High Wycombe; 86 people and only one beginner! Thankfully Terry Eagan, the intrepid leader of the Rock-Hoppers was a BASI instructor himself, and he took our beginner for the first two days until she could join the next class up; Terry was a good friend to us."

"They were great times," said Chris, "snow and sunshine later in the year was a magical combination. I shall continue to tell you about a typical week's ski course. There was a cooked breakfast every day, always porridge and always plenty of toast on the table. Straight after that, the packed lunch trays appeared; loads of jars of peanut butter, chocolate spread of course, and other stuff, chocolate biscuits and lots of fruit. Then off to ski we would go.

The beginners in the Hostel garden, or to the Hayfield, or up the forestry track behind the Hostel. Those who had skied before went up the hill, but Sunday was always busy, so we took things very gently, and allowed them time to find their feet again. On Sunday evening, before dinner, we would issue everyone with a lift pass for the week."

"And so the week went on. On Tuesday evening we would take everyone either swimming, or skating at the Coylumbridge Hotel's outdoor ice rink. What marvellous times we had there; one particular evening it was snowing very heavily, and the A9 blocked. The Hotel had conference people coming, who could not get there, so the chefs brought out to us most of the barbecue they had prepared, steaks, chops, sausages, the lot. The ski course certainly appreciated it! Many lasting friendships developed at that ice rink.

On Wednesday or Thursday we would present Dennis's famous slide show. It showed Glenmore and the Cairngorm mountains in summer and winter, and it certainly persuaded many 'winter people' to come back in the summertime.

But on Friday nights we continued an old Glenmore Lodge tradition, and Plum would lead a grand ceilidh in the dining room. We would dance until we were all exhausted. We always began with the 'Loch Morlich Ski Dance', which everyone took part in, and then dances of all sorts. As time went on, we had dance groups and even Morris men on the course, so we were forever adding to our list of dances as they would teach us. It was a fitting end to a week of great fun."

We moved into the common room and sat down on the comfortable chairs. It was Billy who took up the conversation. "I am certain," he said "that as we ran these ski courses year upon year, they became progressively busier; the coach we used even became a double-decker bus by the end times. But surely we did not operate in isolation? Surely we were just a part of a bigger scene?"

"Oh, Indeed," said Rab "at one time there were fourteen ski schools in this valley. If you like, I can tell you now about the incredible growth of the ski industry, of the development of this valley to accommodate it, and the great mood of optimism and excitement which was all around."

We settled down in our chairs to hear the story. "What a time it was," he began. "In the autumn of 1964 important personages came to Aviemore; Lord and Lady Rank visited in September, and Sir Hugh Fraser and Sir William McEwen Younger came in November. It was of course the Rank organisation which built the Coylumbridge Hotel in 1965. 'A heathery bank will screen it from the road.' exclaimed the Strathy. Then in December 1966 Lady Fraser (Sir Hugh had died by then) opened the £2.5 million Aviemore Centre. 650 guests attended the opening, Sir William McEwen Younger gave an address, praising the late Lord Fraser. He had been 2nd Baron Fraser of Allander, and the main square in the Aviemore Centre is called Allander Square to this day."

"It was also in the early 1960's that the main developments of the ski road took place, transforming it from little better than a forestry track, through a single-track road with passing places to the ashphalt road of today. It is probably a story in itself, but I can tell you that they developed it in three stages, Aviemore to Coylumbridge, Coylumbridge to Glenmore, and from Glenmore up the mountain, four zig-zags taking it up the steepest section. This was after lengthy discussions about the option of starting the chairlift in Aviemore." He smiled. "And after a proposal to build a roof over the section most likely to block with snow; they decided that a £10,000 Swiss snow-blowing machine was a better and cheaper option. Meanwhile Mr Utsi suggested that none of this was necessary, and that his reindeer could pull the people up on sledges!" "On a Saturday in July 1960, the first count was made of cars using the three mile section from the newly opened Loch Morlich Youth Hostel up the mountain; 350 cars used it, even though the new road had not been officially opened."

"Best of all from our point of view, they built the chairlift on Cairngorm, or at least the top half of it," he grinned. "The 'Scotsman' newspaper of 23 December 1961 waxed lyrical about it: 'EXCELSIOR ON CAIRNGORM' it proudly proclaimed."

"They built it from the middle of the mountain to the shoulder near the top, 1100 yards long, so that skiers could easily access the White Lady, Coire Cas via the Traverse, and also Coire na Ciste. Sir Francis Walker of Leys performed the official opening, and he paid tribute to the men who had worked so hard to make it a reality. Herr Gerhard Muller of Zurich was the technical expert, but Archie Scott, Bob Clyde, Tom Paul and Harry MacKay were greatly and duly honoured."

"How, then, did people get from the car park up to the start of the Chairlift?" asked Rosie.

"Well," he replied, "we had to wait until 1964 before the lower section was built, (at a cost of £30,000) which extended it from the middle to nearly the car park, though many people will testify to the very steep and often icy slope you still had to navigate to reach it! However, as for the years in between, I shall let the Scotsman article tell the story: 'From the car park at the end of the ski road it takes about ten to fifteen minutes to get to the White Lady Sheiling. There is a private road owned by the Board which gives access to the sheiling for goods vehicles, but is closed to cars and buses. It makes walking easy, however, and it is not a bad thing to stretch your legs and warm up before starting to ski'!"

"That is not quite correct", I said, "because it is within my memory and the memories of others that Smiths buses, which preceded the Highland Omnibus, would take people up that road to the chairlift station."

"As for the White Lady Sheiling", said Chris, "I shall take up the story there. In the spring of 1948, Jean McIntyre Smith was killed in an accident in Coire Cas; her father, a Hebridean doctor, decided to erect a shelter in her memory. In the autumn of 1951 a firm in Glasgow sent a pre-fabricated hut by lorry to the far end of Loch Morlich. From there the project was co-ordinated by Glenmore Lodge; the sections were hauled by sledges through the forest, over steep glacial moraine, and into Coire Cas. In August Glenmore Lodge staff prepared the site and laid concrete foundations, and the rest of the work was done by parties of 15- and 16-year old kids from Glasgow and Lanarkshire, who were on outdoor training courses at the Lodge, as two carpenters came up from Glasgow to supervise them. Jeans Hut, then, provided shelter for all in Coire Cas until the chairlift came along in 1961, and it was replaced by a two-storey building, the White Lady Sheiling, where many many people will remember eating their packed lunch among crowds of skiers. Jeans Hut was not destroyed, though; Molly and Joe Porter organised yet more parties of school kids from Glasgow and from George Watsons College, and with the help of Bill Blackwood and his tractor, they moved it from Coire Cas into Coire-an-Lochain, where it stood for many more years, being used mainly by climbers."

"Of course", said Billy, "as soon as the chairlift was built, rope tows began to appear, usually run by private operators, in fact, the afore-mentioned Bill Blackwood operated rope-tows in the Ptarmigan bowl and in what we all knew as 'Acacia Avenue'. But as time went by every main run was provided with a T-Bar lift or a poma."

"What I remember", said Rab, laughing, "was that for a while the Car-Park T-Bar ran all the way up to the middle, and that included a section which went rather steeply DOWNhill; many folk fell off there, and you would sometimes find yourself ahead of the lift which was taking you up!"

I thought it was time to offer my ski-teacher friends some light refreshment before dinner, and they readily accepted. Gathering chairs around a table, we soon felt ready to continue the wonderful story, and our original orator took up his tale again.

"I must repeat, it was such a time of great excitement, and I must also say that the infamous £50 foreign travel allowance of Harold Wilson's Government had much to do with bringing this beautiful valley to the nation's attention. It may be surprising enough to know that British Railways began to offer cut-price tickets to Aviemore, but what may truly astonish you is that for a while at least, serious consideration was given to the building of airstrips, in Glen Feshie and in Lochaber!"

"Well, I can certainly tell you", said Rosie, "that in January 1965 British Eagle Airlines offered flights from Birmingham for week-end skiers, all being collected at the airport and taken to the Nethybridge Hotel. The price of which", she giggled, "was £21!"

"We even made it onto a set of stamps!" said Billy, as he placed a set on the table in front of us. "These are 'Landscapes', issued on the second of May 1966. Can you see? the 1s6d stamp has the Queen's head on it of course, and also a picture of the Lairig Ghru and the Cairngorms."

Rab held his hand up for our attention, and he looked thoughtful. "Many people will suppose that 'Monarch of the Glen' was the first and only programme to be filmed in our area; I can tell them they would be wrong!"

"Why is that?" we all asked him.

"They spent five weeks around here in 1966 filming for a childrens' TV programme called 'Ambush at Devils Gap'. It began not at Glenbogle, but at Aviemore station, as the McAllister family arrived for a winter sports holiday. The star was a boy called Mokey. The press release said this: 'Whilst on a winter sports holiday in the Highlands, 5 children encounter an eccentric professor, and quickly find themselves involved in a web of industrial espionage'."

"Now *that*", I suggested "should be well worth re-viewing! But we should perhaps return to telling our story of ski-ing development, in which our Youth Hostel played such a big part."

"Quite so" said Rab, "Here we are from the 'Strathy' in 1964: 'The switching of the British ski-ing championships from Andermatt to the Cairngorms because of the new currency restrictions should bring a big increase in visitors, and will give Scotland a fine opportunity to establish itself as a permanent winter sports centre'."

"It certainly did," said Billy, "in February of that year more than 100 skiers entered for a grand slalom organised by the Aberdeen ski club, with a prize of a pair of Blizzard skis for the winner! The race was shown on Grampian TV. At Easter of the same year more than 3,000 skiers enjoyed what the 'Strathy' described as 'first class ski-ing'."

"Races brought international visitors as well," said Rab. "In March 1966 the Grampian Trophy was held in Coire na Ciste on a 32-gate course set by Karl Fuchs. It was won by Arthur Brugger of Switzerland, and Swiss and Austrians finished second and third. It was very good to note, though, that the leading women were Helen Jamieson and Lindsay Bruce, both of the Dundee Ski Club."

"Hooray for the women, then." said Rosie "but we did make sure we helped our home-grown talent to develop. 16 year old Rory MacLeod from Rothiemurchus was the first recipient of a £300 ski scholarship sponsored by Tomatin Distillers."

"Yes," replied Rab, "in 1966 Iain Finlayson and Fraser Clyde won two of the four £100 Maggi training scholarships after the Scottish Junior Ski Championships were held in 'splendid conditions'. At New Year, remarkably, our local newspaper reported 'Skiers galore on Cairngorm on Monday night, in bright moonlight'!"

"I've got a great one for you all here," said Billy, smiling, and he drew us closer around the table. "In 1966 we held the first, indeed the only Scottish DIATHLON, or 'Sailski event' as it became known to posterity.

T'was in the month of April that the Bearsden Ski Club and the Helensburgh Sailing Club jointly issued a challenge to the Dundee Ski Club and the Royal Tay Yacht Club. That challenge was eagerly accepted, and early in the merry month of May, 16 intrepid mariners and skiers made their way to our Glen, the idea being that one or perhaps two yachting races on Loch Morlich on the Saturday, plus a slalom race on the White Lady on the Sunday should settle the issue. Under a sunny and cloudless sky, with a warm, gusty SW wind, they dragged the boats onto the beach at Loch Morlich. The dauntless Captains were Bruce Benson for the West, and Hugh Scott for the East.

On arriving at the beach they made two discoveries. The first, as so many people have discovered since, was that the water in Loch Morlich in early spring is icy cold, being the main receptacle for the melting snow. The second was that nobody had quite decided what the exact rules should be. The decision was taken that the new bar at the Coylumbridge Hotel was obviously the best place to sort this out, and off they went. Having returned and organised the rescue boat, they realised that all that remained was to finalise the scoring system, so back to the bar it was.

Eventually racing took place, the names of the combattants having now passed into legend. On the sailing side, there was Donald McClaren, Christopher Stuart-Corry and Per Formo from Norway. Some of the notable skiers were George Bruce, Hamish Liddell and Gavin Ogilvie.

When it came down to it, the issue was this: could the superior Helensburgh sailors win by a sufficient margin to compensate for Dundee's superiority on skis? In the end they could not, and the SailSki trophy was presented to the victorious East team by the

Glasgow Herald. A legend in his own lifetime, Bob Benzies was there to report the whole thing.

I call now upon the Ironmen and Tri-athletes of today to accord due honour to the noble deeds of their predecessors; we did it here first!"

"Wonderful", said Rosie, "but we ought now to tell of the story of ski instruction here. As more and more people came here to learn, instructors were needed, and Norwegian, Swiss and Austrian techniques were being taught at the same time as young Scots were training to become teachers.

It was Moray and Nairn Education Committee who described the demand for a ski instructor scheme as 'overwhelming'. And so, on Friday 22 March 1963, BAPSI was formed."

"British Association of Professional Ski Instructors" added Chris, "and they dropped the 'P' and made it into BASI in 1967."

"Quite," said Rosie "Frith Finlayson was very much the main man, and the first trainers were Jack Thomson, Karl Fuchs and Robin Stephens. They decided on a format of training for one week, followed by a two-day examination. Glenmore Lodge was the base of operations, and Eric Langmuir, the Principal seemed well pleased, he described one Easter course where the candidates 'skied every day, from dawn till dusk'."

"At the same time, Derek Brightman and Sandy Caird formed the Aviemore Ski School, and it was the hotels (and Youth Hostels) who were involved from the start." said Chris.

"Yes indeed" said Rab, "it was the Nethybridge Hotel which provided a grand dinner for no less a personage than Arne Palm from Geilo, the Chief Director of Ski Instruction in Norway; the hotel was also the venue for the first ever 3-day ski conference. Arne Palm was 'most impressed' by the standard of instruction, and was 'tremendously impressed by the potential for development'. He suggested that Slochd would be a suitable place for even further development."

"The ski schools involved in that first conference were these:" said Rosie "Scottish Norwegian, Nethybridge Hotel, Austrian, Carrbridge Hotel, Boat of Garten Hotel, Badenoch, Coylumbridge Hotel, Aviemore, Glenshee, Glencoe, the Angus Hotel in Blairgowrie, and, of course, the SYHA. So we were involved right from the start; our representative, and our first Chief Instructor was Robin Stephens."

"Robin's early life took him to many parts of the world, including Antartica; his love for ski-ing led him to several trips to Norway, and at least one trip to Austria, with Derek Brightman."

"That must have been something really worth watching," I interjected "Derek to this day holds BASI qualification licence number ONE, and Robin gained the highest Norwegian Ski-Laerer qualification, the first British skier to do so!"

Rosie took up the story again: "The time came when Robin arrived at the SYHA's remarkable roundhouse building at Glenisla, in the company of 'the irascible Toby Riesing'. At nearby Glenshee and with the help of some other Norwegians who were studying at Herriot-Watt College, they taught pupils and issued them with Norwegian star proficiency badges 1, 2 and 3.
Rab Smith arrived at Glenisla too, and took an instructors course with Robin," She laughed, "He remembers just what all of us will remember too, and so will many of our pupils: 'typical eye-watering icy winds, and skis chattering across blue ice'."

Chris smiled. "Yes, Rab had his own inimitable way of describing the early equipment as well: 'Skis looked like they had been carved from solid trees, Kandahar bindings pretended to have a release system, but stretched a few achilles in their time, and boots...I had a pair of red leather multipurpose walking/ski-ing boots whose curved soles made minimum contact with the flat ski. From ankle-cracking Kandahar bindings, we jumped to Marker turntables that might have been safer, but for the "longthong" we strapped on to make sure that no boot would ever release, even if corkscrewed in a 360 degree twirling crash'."

"Thus prepared and equipped, our dauntless instructors set off for Loch Morlich, to begin the great adventure." I said. "Arthur Cromar was General Secretary by then, and a very well known skier before that, so he took a keen interest in the development, on several occasions driving Robin from Glenisla to Glenmore, (and twice having to turn back because of snow at Drumochter). Robin was full-time Chief Instructor now, ski-ing at Loch Morlich, sailing at Tighnabruaich and giving publicity lectures in the autumn, based at Bruntsfield."

"And so it came to pass," said Rosie "that the team of our earliest predecessors finally assembled at Loch Morlich Youth Hostel, and their names will surely pass into legend."

"Robin was Chief Instructor; there was big Ron McLelland, there was Billy MacLean, Rab Smith, and two girls, MA Harper and Pam Hammond. Robin married Kath, whom he met when she came on a ski course!" She raised her eyebrows and smiled, "perhaps the first, but by no means the last time *THAT* happened! After a few years working for SYHA they moved on and took over the running of Tighnabruaich Sailing School, where they settled happily. Ron McLelland had a few adventures and mis-adventures at Loch Morlich, then he married Joanne and they went to live happily ever after in New Zealand. Billy stayed for a couple of years; it was MA herself who remembered that they were ski-ing in what we used to call the 'sugar bowl', Billy noticed a snowplough on the ski road and promptly thought it would be a challenge to ski down from the slope above and jump it! He broke his leg. He moved to Oban, and started his own sailing school there. Rab Smith's main claim to fame is that he took no less a legend than Archie Fisher for his first day on skis; he married another Pamela, and in 1966 they too moved to South Island, New Zealand. They keep in touch still with Ron and his wife, Rab also came back to visit his old haunts in Glenmore in 2010.

To tell the stories of the two girls would take another book; Pam worked for one season with Hans Kuwall in Carrbridge, and then both girls set off to explore the remoter parts of the world, including Nagaland and the Chilean Andes. Pam was a guide for Bales Tours, who specialise in that sort of thing; MA led for Sherpa, Exodus and Himalayan Kingdoms. MA is currently writing a book about her drive to India and back!"

"Yes," I said "MA contacted me last year and casually mentioned that she was staying with Pam and then both were setting off for Cuba. Interesting what other snippets she remembered from so long ago: they were paid £7 14 shillings a week, and MA reckoned she spent most of it on biscuits and cheese! To operate the hostel showers, you had to put a penny in the slot; and she drove a blue VW Beetle, UWS 898. She also remembers that the ski courses were fed in the staff room, by Mrs Bull."

"There is some evidence," said Rosie "that the male members of this team shamelessly told departing nurses and other female ski course members of the prizes they were offering for a baking competition, for fudge, cakes and other delicious goodies. A steady stream of tasty treats certainly arrived to sustain their sugar levels throughout the winter."

Amid general laughter, Billy took up the tale. "Interesting, that each and every one of these folk well remember walking up to Coire Cas carrying all their gear, sometimes camping at the snow-line. What a blessing it was, when they built the ski road and chairlift."

"Before we get another round of drinks and snacks" I said, "I just want to talk to you for a minute about a different subject, but one which is dear to all our hearts, we who dauntlessly took our ski-courses out, whatever the weather!. In August 1960, a 300 yard section of the ski road was simply swept away by a sudden cloudburst; 40 people were trapped above the gap by 'raging floodwaters', and were rescued later that night by a human chain. The following January, a severe blizzard blocked the road and the railway line, bus services were cancelled, and cars were abandoned. The next year the Strathspey railway line was undermined, roads damaged, crops battered and flattened by a cloudburst which sent floodwaters cascading down the mountainside, carring trees and boulders, and destroying in their path all the repair work done on the road previously. A severe blizzard in 1965 led the 'Strathy' to proclaim: 'Stormbound Strathspey', and described the building of the chairlift as having taken place 'despite persistently foul weather, gales, sleet and snow have contrived against the workmen, but they have been magnificent continuing to work in winds that you could lean against'."

"Then perhaps we were 'magnificent' too, often enough." said Chris. "Let us have some more drinks."

We settled again, and it was Billy who continued the story. "Instructors, of course, came and went, some stayed for longer than others. I remember Gordon Tiley, Christopher Martin, Alex Ferguson."

"MA taught ski-ing with Christopher for one season in Valmorel" said Chris, "he married a 'new age' girl and went off to live in Esalen, near San Francisco."

"Gordon shared his time betwen instructing here and running his engineering business in Bristol. Isobel and Peter were others who were part-time teachers."

"Alex held high office in SYHA, but he taught ski-ing as well." I said. "He was one of many who had skied in Geilo in Norway, and the hostel always maintained its close links with Norway. He was part of the Glenisla link also; he instructed at Loch Morlich in 1964 and 1965, then at Glenisla in 1966 and 1967. And, he was another early member of the Loch Morlich marriage bureau; in 1970 he married Jennifer, who was assistant warden."

A short period of thoughtful silence. "Joe Docherty and Watty Lester" I prompted. "I mention them because I will always remember them as being extremely kind men, and each helped me along the road between being a skier and becoming an instructor."

"Joe was another man from the Clydeside shipyards" said Rosie, "he stayed for quite a while with the hostel, teaching his classes with a very easy style, and would always have a kind word for you. All the while he was content to live in a caravan on Dalfaber Road."

"Walter (Watty) Lester followed in the tradition of being a skier and a sailor. He taught with us for a couple of seasons, and also worked with Elif Moen at the Scottish Norwegian Ski School. He would spend his summers up in Ullapool, teaching the basics of seamanship and sailing out to the Summer Isles; quite an idyllic life. He also was a great help to Clive Freshwater when he was building his place at Loch Insh."

"Our links with Glenisla were maintained during the hectic years when David (and Aggie) Dalrymple and their protoge Alex Snaddon came to join us" said Billy. "It always seemed to me that the pace of life was so much faster in those halcyon days, and the ski courses were getting busier all the time. Never any shortage of snow then." he mused thoughtfully. "And then, in the summer, they would go off to that round building in the idyllic setting of Kirkton of Glenisla, and would run courses for the SYHA, pony trekking and archery, and canoeing and sailing on Loch Shandra - what a place of great beauty that was, on a long summer evening."

"Harry Jamieson was a real stalwart of the earlier days" said Rosie, "stayed for quite a few years. He married a Swiss girl,

Christianne; they stayed in the hostel for a short while after that. Harry then moved to Nethybridge and made a very good business for himself selling fishing rods."

I wandered over to the window and gazed wistfully at the majestic mountains in the distance. "You know, I really cannot believe now that I was once as fit as that; at the end of the ski season, when the weather was more likely to be good, Plum took Harry, myself, and Carolyn up to Cairngorm summit. We skied down Coire Raibert (and by the way this was on downhill skis, not touring ones) and the we SIDE-STEPPED up to Ben Macdui. Of course, the run down from there right the way back to the hostel made it all worthwhile, and I have an abiding memory of Harry suddenly veering off and shooting down the side-wall of Coire-an-Lochain in the tuck position, to get enough speed to carry him out at the end; he finished up a long way ahead of the rest of us. We did that for two seasons running."

"We were very pleased" I added, "to have Jeff Faulkner teach for us for a couple of seasons. A strong skier, always good with his pupils and brought them on well. His wife Margaret became friends with Patricia."

"Good with his pupils" laughed Rosie, "until two Indian doctors got the better of him. Try as they might, they could not master riding up the T-bars. In desperation, rather than a lack of gallantry, he passed them over to the care of Marian Burrows-Smith, who also was helping out at that time. Even her feminine charms and expertise failed with these two, and one of them decided that it was easier for him to walk up Coire Cas!"

Billy grinned. "So, what about the girls?" he asked.

"Well," replied Rab, "MA and Pam were a hard act to follow I admit, but our female instructors who followed after certainly kept the standards very high, and we are deeply grateful to every one of them."

"Anna Cook arrived with Tom in their beat-up VW campervan late one autumn afternoon. They had already travelled half way around the world in it, from their home in New Zealand; they decided to stay and we are glad that they did. Anna held a New Zealand ski-instructors' badge, and she joined the staff. That coincided with the arrival of the mercurial Iain Baxter onto our team. They quickly discovered that they shared a love of racing, and many an afternoon saw slalom poles pushed into the ice and snow on the steep slope above the Fiacaill ski run. The crisis came when Anna beat Iain's time in the instructors' race on the White Lady, but they remained firm friends with much mutual respect."

"And that, even though she had borrowed Iain's own skis for the race, he having an earlier start time. That left him completely without excuse." I chuckled. "At the end of the season we agreed to swap badges, and I was proud to wear a Kiwi instructor's badge for several seasons."

"After that," said Rab, "Anna spent many years guiding in the Indian Himalayas, taking tours and Heli-ski guiding. She returned home to South Island, took up snow-kiting, and lives now with her partner Dave on the shores of the idyllic Lake Hawea, Central Otago."

"Chrissie Clyde was the wife of Bob Clyde, the chairlift manager," said Rosie "it was just delightful when she came to work with us. She was there at the same time as Robin Guy, Carolyn Malam and Joe Burns. She was such a neat skier, with a greater-than-usual gift for making ski-ing look easy. It was always the females in her classes who responded best to her, perhaps she was ahead of her time?"

"She also shared great mutual respect and affection for my auntie Patricia" I said, "she was no stranger to helping with the washing-up in the kitchen, or even helping with breakfasts and packed lunches."

"Rosie Grayson came to join us in the earlier days as well," said Rab "she was from Long Eaton in the east midlands and was a teacher at Bramcote Hills School; Paul Booth was around at that time, too. Rosie was a quiet girl, often she would sit in the staff room in the evening, doing her knitting."

"Kathy Murgatroyd came to us from Ski School d'Ecosse; she could hold her own with MA and Pam when it came to mountains. She was the first female to do what Hamish Brown did: climb all the Munros in a single trip. She moved on to Taynault and continued her outdoor life there, sailing and horse-riding."

"Marion Wilke, a local girl, came to join us; she was another fast skier who was interested in racing. Then, after Plum retired and Jim McDowall took over as Chief Instructor, we were joined by Nicky Clift, the girl from Slaley in Northumberland, and Bronwen Crymble, wife of Sam Crymble a great climber who worked at Glenmore Lodge. Now Bronwen's job within the ski school was to look after all the cross-country skiers, and she would take them up along the forest tracks when snow allowed, which it often did. Doug Godlington helped us out for one memorable week with that as well; his class came back every night soaked to the skin and sore with laughter; they had been shaking the snow off the trees with their ski poles, and of course on top of the one behind. But cross-country takes us on to another story," said Rab.

"It certainly does," I said "do you know, during all my time at the Loch Morlich ski school we never saw the rise of snow-boarding. What we did witness was a tremendous rise in the number of people who wanted to learn cross-country ski-ing. That led to the arrival in Glenmore of Bob Douglas. You might say of Bob that he was a man of many talents. He would not call himself a professional photographer, but his work certainly of that standard, and he was able to sell photographs to outdoor magazines and such like. He had trained in Norway, in biathlon, and he was used to ski-ing with a rifle on his back. Certainly, when he put his racing skis on here, which were almost as thin as ice skate blades, he could ski with bewildering speed. And yet he had a great gift of patience, and an ability to demonstrate moves with great precision. This meant that he was ideally equipped to become a ski teacher of the highest standard. If he could find a flat, open field of snow in the forest, he would persuade his class to help him make a checker-board pattern in the snow. Thus, holding his poles half-way along and carrying them parallel to the ground, he would demonstrate to his class by ski-ing across their front, then towards them, then away from them. That way, the usual beginners shuffle forwards was rapidly turned into a glide, which itself became longer and better balanced as time progressed. Bob certainly produced many quite elegant cross-country skiers during his time with us. When he left us, he went to the Lake District and took up fell-running."

"It was at this time that Bill Wilson joined the team, primarily as a downhill instructor. Bob, though, increased Bill's interest in cross-country ski-ing to the extent that he later wrote a book about telemark ski-ing. The two became firm friends, and Plum often mentioned, 'the Bill and Bob Show'."

"Two more 'men of the mountains' joined us under Jim McDowall" said Rab. "Jim Briggs and Mike Watts. Jim worked also as a ranger for Rothiemurchus estate; Mike travelled the wide world, sailing and ski-ing wherever he could."

Billy grinned. "We really should go and join the others now, and prepare for this sumptuous dinner." He held up his hand. "But absolutely not before we drink a toast to a great man, a man to whom we all owe such a great debt, and a man, without whom none of this would have been possible." We raised our glasses. "To Norman 'Plum' Worrall!"

"His roots were in the city of Manchester, where he briefly followed his trade as a plumber, hence the nick-name by which he was affectionately known all his life. First and foremost he thought of himself as a painter. He was good enough to have had exhibits in galleries, even at the Tate once. He painted what he saw all through his career; after he retired from instructing, he would go off with his wife Nan in his old campervan, with the intention, as he once told me, to paint every glen in Scotland. I once met him in Watestones, well into old age and with his hands shaking violently. I asked why he was buying paints. 'You see, John-dogs,' (his voice was always gentle, sometimes tender) 'as soon as my hand touches the paper, the shaking stops and I will always paint'. And so he did. He presented me with two of his paintings as my wedding present, and I tell you, they are my prized possessions now."

"He was a climber too." prompted Rosie. "That he certainly was,' I said "He was a founder member of the Karabiner Climbing Club in Manchester in 1944; he was very keen that the club should be of mixed gender, unusual for those days, but it may have had something to do with his wife, Robbie! Many of his mates remember him from days on the Derbyshire and Lakeland hills. But his love of mountains brought him north, and to this valley. He went first to join the Austrian ski school at Carrbridge, and Plum became the first British man to gain an Austrian ski-lehrer qualification from no less a legend than Karl Fuchs himself. Then he worked for many years at Glenmore Lodge as a climbing instructor as well as a ski teacher. One hosteller, Peter Ball, told me he could remember coming in 1958 in his converted A30 van; he went climbing in Coire-an-t-Sneachda with a group, and the only name that he could remember was Plum."

"His first wife was Martha," said Chris "but everybody knew her as 'Robbie'. She died in 1963, and he later married Nan and they danced and skied their lives together. Everybody knew that they lived in Kinveachy Gardens, Aviemore."

66

"But he was so much at home in the mountains." I said. "Which of his many special gifts should we talk about first? Some described it as a 6th sense, but I think it was a very special memory; many people could testify to going on long treks with him, in atricious weather, and feeling lost, yet every one of them would agree that they felt that Plum knew exactly where they were at any given time. And surely all of us can remember that, late in the ski season Plum could effortlessly point out to us where the best area might be for what we were teaching; that was because he had a photographic memory of how and where the snow had first fallen in December."

"Perfect balance and infinite patience" suggested Rosie. "It was the combination of those two which made him such a supremely gifted ski teacher, as I think every one of his pupils would recognise," I said "but I think you woud have to add to that a wealth of experience. He was involved from the earliest days, from days when folk considered whether Braeriach or Cairngorm would be the better mountain to develop for ski-ing. He himself told me that he used to walk up Sron na Lairig (the approach to Braeriach) so that he could ski down its long convex slope; the astonishing thing is that he sometimes had six runs in a day!"

"But I think he really did possess the gift of perfect balance, in the way that a top ballet dancer might have. That is why he went far beyond making ski-ing look easy, he made it look effortless; he could (and often did) perform parallel turns, skis locked tight together, at much slower speeds than most instructors could, and on occasions without his heel binding clipped down."

"And that is also why he was able to dance so well - and for so long. It was Plum who carried on the tradition from Glenmore Lodge days of holding a ceilidh on a Friday night; he would lead every dance during the evening and not really be out of breath. It was he who invented what became the traditional opening dance: the Loch Morlich ski dance. And Nan, a very good dancer herself, could surely testify, at New Year and other big occasions Plum would take her to a dinner dance and keep her on her feet all night."

"Whenever conditions allowed, and especially later in the season, Plum would have no hesitation in ski-ing everybody back to the hostel at the end of the day. Sometimes by the side of the road, when the traffic was at a standstill. That would lead us onto the old zig-zags, which was really good ski-ing if the snow had drifted into it. Once, when leading my class, we side-slipped off the road onto those zig-zags and suddenly realised that the whole slope was sliding too! A miniature avalanche, only about twenty gentle yards, but it was an unreal experience. If everybody could ski really well, Plum would lead us up the Ptarmigan tow and down the ridge above Coire na Ciste. Then we would swing right and would go swooping into Coire Loaigh Mhor and out again, at death-defying speeds, or so it seemed. That would bring us onto the Coire na Ciste road, and it was then that Plum would come into his own. We would ski gently down the easy slope between the road and the forest, and then Plum would know exactly where to turn off into the trees, and there the adventure began. The track was narrow, - snowploughs were not a realistic option - and in parts quite steep. It was not unknown for people to grab hold of a tree to slow themselves down. That, of course, would bring lots of snow from the top of that tree down onto those behind. But we always arrived safely onto the forestry track at the bottom, nursing our wounds and listening to the rest of the party as they came careering and crashing through the forest. From there it was over the bridge and an easy coast back to the hostel."

"Stories about him abound" said Rab. "They certainly do," I said "these are all being gathered, together with his life story into a book by Doug Godlington; it is going to be called 'Chasing Snowflakes'. In fact, if you will, I can tell you now a story which

has not yet been told; a story of how Doug and Plum first met!"
Everyone gathered round, a little closer.

"Early Derbyshire days. Doug and a group of friends used to make use of a hut on the south side of Kinder, and would cycle up, carrying skis on their bikes, and go hunting for snow patches. This particular week-end, most of the snow had drifted up against the dry-stone walls. They soon noticed, on the other side of the Snake Pass a long patch of snow 20 to 30 yards wide, They made their way to it, and became aware that other skiers were already there. One man in particular was ski-ing towards them, long, graceful, sweeping turns, and carrying a small dog in his arms. He approached Doug's group with a cheery 'Hellooo', and as he approached the dry-stone wall at the bottom, the snow gave way beneath him. Plum ended up cart-wheeling over the wall and disappeared into the drift on the other side. The dog was propelled into the air, and Doug describes it as if in slow-motion on a video, the dog 'walking' frantically in mid-air until it made a graceful landing next to Doug's group. Plum emerged, feet first from the drift and made his usual exclamation: 'Bloody hell, where's my dog finished up? Is he still in the snowdrift?'."

"Another thing that Doug remembers well is being in the upper floor of the Sheiling with Plum, HRH Prince Charles and of course his bodyguard, Plum had been teaching the Prince to ski in the Ptarmigan bowl at the top and had managed to ski him safely down to the middle. That was in the Prince's Gordonstoun days. On a later visit, when Charles was followed by a pack of press photographers, Plum took a decoy, dressed just like the Prince with him, so that Charles could have a lesson in peace."

"Here is a story he told me himself" said Chris. "He was camping in winter with a group of scoolgirls at Loch Etchacan, one of Plum's favourite places. The girls started to play about on the ice. Suddenly a piece broke off with one girl on it, and started to drift away. The girl had two pigtails, so Plum and another instructor, showing great presence of mind, grabbed a pigtail each and steered the girl back to safety."

"Legends persist of him ski-ing all day, complaining he had a blister which was becoming very sore, and then discovering a spark-plug inside his boot; preparing to go walking with a very old pair of boots with holes in, and applying Dubbin to his feet! But I can tell you of the day he went up with the ski bus as usual, then realised he had forgotten his ski boots. He got a lift back down with the bus and came up in his car with his ski boots. At the end of the day he was deep in conversation with several members of his class and got on the bus happily telling them tales of ski-ing in remote areas of the world. He got back into the hostel kitchen and as usual made his cup of tea with a very unsteady hand, and then realised his car was still up in the car park."

"His nephew, Dave Fairhurst, and myself, and several others can tell you from personal experience, how scary it could be to get in his car with him. Dave tells of, 'coming down from the hill when he was driving below 40 mph in first gear, getting everyone's attention, careering all over the road as he tried to light his pipe, then dropping the lit match and frantically trying to put it out.' I myself remember once getting a lift with him along the side of Loch Morlich. He was indeed driving very slowly, but in first gear; he had a habit of leaning further and further towards you when he was deep in conversation. On this occasion he was explaining to me the finer points of parallel turns; first one hand came off the steering wheel to demonstrate to me, then the other one as he moved both hands in a graceful parallel turn! All I could see was the car moving ever closer towards the loch."

"His dog was called Ceildh" said Chris, "he would chase 'bun-rabs' as Plum always called them. Plum used to buy the family meat for the freezer, by asking the butcher to chop enough joints to last him about a month. Legend has it in Aviemore that he went one day to get the meat while Nan took Ceilidh for a walk. Plum bought the meat, put it into the boot of the car and went off to look for Nan. Meanwhile Nan returned, wondering where he was, so she put Ceildh into the back of the car and went off to find Plum. Ceildh did not need to chase 'bun-rabs' for weeks after that!"

"We must be sure," I said "that we remember him as infinitely more than just a figure of fun. One day, ski-ing in a school holiday, I vivdly remember looking up, seeing on the chairlift a large man, wearing a cap and with glasses, smoking a pipe. Underneath the chair a dog was running, carrying one of his ski poles. I did not know at that time just how large a part that man would play in my life, nor could I guess how he would endear himself, as he touched their lives, to countless hundreds of others."

King Haakon VII
entering the old
front door.

The Norwegian
King and
Officers of
Kompani Linge

The Norwegian Huts.

Re-union 1973

The original Warden's Office, now the Quiet Room.

Dennis, Glen and Sally in Glen Feshie

Dennis in his 'pomp', half way down Coire Raibert.

Patricia hard at work in her kitchen.

Walter Lester; everyone knew him as 'Watty'.

Plum, Ian Baxter, Anna Cook. No snow in sight!

Plum and Kathy Murgatroyd on the famous ski bus.

Jim McDowall and his SYHA instructors team, 1980's.

Dennis with
Paul
Richardson,
Assistant
Warden.

Gaile Bryson,
Jennifer Curtis

The ones with
4 legs are the
Reindeer!

Glenmore youngsters in the hostel garden.

Hostel 1963. Note the twin Cypress trees.

The Assistants; Their Tale

We meandered thoughtfully back towards the others in the staff room. On the way I pushed open the door of the dining room. A room about two thirds wide as it was long; to the left, a large serving hatch from the kitchen; to the right three large windows offered stunning views of the ridge of the northern Cairngorms. Long tables and plastic chairs were stacked in one corner.

I glanced down at the floor and said to the others: "This is where all the Friday night ceilidhs we were talking about took place. The floor was very forgiving" "I bet that is not what the assistants thought when they swept, mopped and polished it on the Saturday morning" said Chris.

"It was my Auntie," I said, ignoring that comment "who provided the music, she put her turntable deck onto the shelf next to the hatch in the kitchen, and we had three or four LPs with the right music for each dance marked on the record sleeves. We prided ourselves that we did a very presentable eightsome reel."

We moved out and turned right into the washing up kitchen. A large square room, along the left wall were floor cupboards with a wide shelf, and above were glass cupboards full of plates and saucers. The main feature of the shelf was a large 'Bonzer' can opener at one end. In the centre was a unit with four large sinks. "That is where the hostellers did the washing up" I said.

We moved into the kitchen. To our right, two walk-in cupboards and a large fridge, to our left a shelf containing two large sinks where, it must be admitted, for many years two or three chosen hostellers would help to peel the tatties. On the opposite side was a double gas cooker, two large ovens and eight gas rings. To the left, a larger gas ring was set lower down. To the right, a deep fat fryer. Looking towards the dining room was the serving hatch and on the right of that another large shelf with two electric toasters, and several toast racks made from old skis.

I turned my gaze, wistfully, towards the back door. It led into a small porch to the outer door, which in turn led you into the back passageway, to the left, the ski room, to the right two large cold store rooms and then outside where there was a large gas tank and then a garage. My uncle always parked his Humber Hawk outside it, I think because it was too wide to fit inside.

It was Rosie who picked up on my gaze. "Are you perhaps reflecting on all the people who came through that door during your years here?" she asked.

"Goodness me," I said "more than I could possibly remember. But it is nice to think that people felt welcome to drop by for a coffee and a chat. Let me see, in the earliest days there was Bill Kerr; he was a telephone linesman from Grantown, but he was also involved with the Cairngorms Rescue Team, and used to tell tales of spending New Year at the Shelter Stone with a bottle of good whisky to protect him from the cold.

Don and Judy Rumbold would talk with Dennis about many things. Malcolm and Ginty Hunt were involved with the ski school, but they were based at Glenmore Lodge. Ian Bishop helped out sometimes with summer and winter courses, but was never averse to a cup of tea and a blether.

But I have to say that of all the vistors, perhaps the most delightful, who used to appear two or three evenings a week, was Johnny the Pole."

The others looked at me quizically. I went on to explain. "When Mrs Reid finished her duties with Glenmore Lodge, she took over the Tea Room at Glenmore Shop, and quickly re-established herself as a living legend. Ham rolls not only contained copious amounts of ham, but the rolls were fresh and always spread with the best butter; hot chocolates were made with all milk and real ground chocolate. Anyway, Patricia had a slicing machine in this kitchen, just behind the door. Johhny had become Mrs Reid's assistant and he would bring up the ham, greet us with a beaming smile and a bow, and would then proceed to slice up the ham to take back to the cafe. What happened afterwards always amazed me. Johnny would finish slicing and pack up the ham. He would then take the slicing machine apart, taking immense care to wash, dry and polish every single piece of it, and re-assemble it, spotlessly clean. Another bow and a barely discernable, 'Thank you, Good night to you' and he was gone."

"I suppose you might say that the most necessary morning visitor was Bella the milk lady, indeed the porridge, essential on cold winter mornings, could hardly have been made without it. At the busiest times it was made in a huge pot on top of the lower gas ring. Bella once had a story in the 'Strathy', when a rainstorm washed away part of the road and her van nearly disappeared down a pothole. She survived that incident, and delivered the milk in huge churns; what a job we had on mornings when it was plenty below and the top was frozen solid. If you wanted milk in your coffee, we could ask you, 'one lump or two?'. In hot summers it was a different problem, and the milk would not keep for long, but Patricia would then use it to make what one of her assistants described as 'the best scones ever'."

"So stirring the porridge was the assistant's job, then?" asked Chris.

"Together with the tea, the coffee, the bacon, the toast and the packed lunch trays, yes it was," I smiled "And I forgot the cereals. There was always plenty to do and Patricia could not have managed without a good kitchen assistant. She herself had a large oval pan, across three of the gas rings and would break 40 or 50 eggs into it to fry them. Over all the years, if I saw her break one yolk, it was a many as she ever did break. After the toast was collected, we would then put a fresh loaf on top of the packed lunch trays made up the night before, and put them out also, for the ski or summer course members to make up their own sandwiches. The lorne sausage acquired the name 'reindeer burger', some saved their bacon and egg for sandwiches, and cheese with chocolate spread became a legend."

"Of course," said Billy "It was at this point that the bus drivers would come in, and often be given a good cooked breakfast served, you might guess, by the kitchen assistant. But the bus drivers have their own story to tell."

"And a little later, the Posties would arrive" I said, "Euan or Sandy usually, and they were not averse to a coffee and a chat if time allowed."

"So, after breakfast and packed lunch had been served, returned, washed up and put away," I said "the next part of a kitchen assistant's day would often be concerned with sleeping sheets. Patricia bought an industrial washing machine (towards which the SYHA made a handsome contribution) and installed it in the washing up kitchen. In the summer it was a very pleasant duty to go up the bank above the garage and peg them out on the long washing lines we had up there. Jennifer Ferguson remembers being paid 6d for each one, and that went towards her £32 per month wages; Sheila Hall remembers having to wash 100 before she could get out one afternoon, and Margaret Franklin remembers them as 'endless' and says that one morning a buzzard landed on the ground right beside her as she was pegging them out."

"The assistant warden, meanwhile, might well have been helping Dennis with the bookings, but the main part of his, or her, work would begin straight after breakfast - giving out the duties to the hostellers. He would do this fully in the knowledge that anything which was not properly cleaned or swept or tidied by the hostellers he would have to do himself later. It would certainly not be appropriate these days, but it was a system which worked well enough in its time, and I certainly never had any concscientious objectors. Some hostels had a written list of duties, some even had printed cards, but I learnt from one of the best, big Jim Williamson from Dundee, who explained to me that it was important to have a good mental picture of what needed to be done each particular day, and to get the hostellers to work together if possible, to feel part of a team."

"Every Saturday, change-over day, we would sweep, mop and polish every floor and would then bring out a remarkably cumbersome machine which we referred to as 'the bumper'. It was supposed to buff the polished floor to produce an even shine, at least that was the theory, but it was incredibly heavy and, especially when there was a tad too much polish, you no sooner nervously pressed the 'ON' switch than you would find yourself dragged to the other side of the room as you frantically tried to switch it off before it ran over your toes. We learned to have fun with it in the end, but not before it had damaged a few bits of furniture by banging into them."

"Did we not alternate closing with Aviemore at the end of summer?" asked Chris.

"Certainly" I replied, "In October and November. We would stay open one of those months while Aviemore closed, and then vice-versa. That was so that there would always be a bed available for travellers at any time. It also gave the wardens a chance for a holiday, but then the task of stripping the hostel and cleaning from top to bottom fell to the assistants. Most memorable at the end of each summer was the sheer amount of sand which came out of each dormitory, from under the matress covers mostly; how people slept was a mystery to me. We would sweep and shovel it all into two or three plastic dustbins and carry it all back to the beach."

We wandered into the staff room and warmly greeted the other guests.

"We were talking about assistants" said Chris, "and those two rooms there were accommodation for them."

"Yes," said Rab, "it was one large room once, but early on it was split into two; good idea, because assistants often worked in pairs, and this was a more private, sheltered area for girls. In the round turret there was a bathroom."

"There is one story I can tell you about that" I said, "of a day on the hill when it had snowed, then rained, then sleet and a high wind, then it snowed again. I got back feeling like a drowning cat. I ran a hot bath, took off my ski boots and jacket, and then got into the bath just as I was, I was so wet it just did not matter."

"Anyway, we perhaps should return to our tale, 'a day in the life of an assistant warden'. Four o'clock, (once upon a time we closed between 11 and 4, but on becoming a busy Grade 1 we only closed 12 until2) saw both assistants on duty. The kitchen assistant might well be seated on the stool we had provided next to the low gas ring. The stirring of the 'soup du jour' was an essential preparation for the evening meal, and the care we took over it meant that it always seemed to be popular, summer and winter. Meanwhile, in the early days, some lucky hostellers might be peeling the tatties in the large sinks in the washing up kitchen, at least until we got the tattie-peeling machine; what a blessing that was."

"When the evening meal was ready" said Chris, "there was the ceremony of the ringing of the great bell to summon the hungry. Usually Patricia's job, but assistants were allocated the task when we were busy."

"The assistant warden, meanwhile, would be behind the office counter. In winter, there was always a queue for the showers, and many of the ski course ventured down to Glenmore Cafe for apple strudel, or creme eggs, or Kendal mint cake. In the long hot days of summer most would stay on the beach or out on the hill until much later, so the office shop would not be very busy until later in the evening, but it was the main time for new arrivals. We had a large register to fill in, several columns wide. One was for sheet sleeping bags, if you did not possess an 'approved' one, we hired one out for a small charge, and on leaving the sheet was returned to be washed (by the kitchen assistant) and we had a record of who had them. Another column, in the early days was for car parking. In 1949, the charge was 1s for cars and 6d for motor cycles; that practice continued into the mid 1960's, becuse the SYHA handbook stated that hostels were for the use of people travelling 'by foot, bicycle or canoe'."

"I can just about remember a charge for cars" said Rab, "it was 1s 6d when I first arrived, but that same handbook had this rule also: 'Silence must be observed between the hours of 11 and 7'."

"It worked at the time" I said. "The register of course was as necessary then as it is now, a record of who is there in case of fire or evacuation. That is in fact another story for later! But we also had racks on the wall of the warden's office, one for each dormitory, and we put everyone's hostel card into them. That was firstly so that we knew who was in which room, and also because at night, the assistant warden's job was to fill in a statistics sheet of which nationalities were staying."

"It was by no means essential, but if any assistant possessed the ability and the willingness to play Canasta, they would be highly regarded by D and P. It is a card game, based on rummy, which requires four players, and as I was usually there to make three, the importance of a Canasta-playing assistant becomes obvious. Entire evenings were spent playing this game, seated around the large kitchen table, sometimes observed by curious cats, and often interrupted by the ring of the bell at the warden's office, by a new arrival or by school kids wanting to buy chocolate bars. To win at

Canasta requires 5,000 points, and Dennis was rarely known to stir from his chair until one pair had reached that total."

We took our seats around the table with the other guests awaiting the great feast. It was Rosie who looked up. "So, what were their names, these young ladies and gentlemen? Who were these assistants who played such a large part in the running of this hostel in its heyday?"

Rab took it up. "Well, I was here probably before any of you, but my memory is playing tricks, and I cannot recall everyone."

"There was a strong connection with Dundee in the early years. Dennis Fagan was the assisitant warden, and he hailed from that 'bonnie' city. Now, possibly before Mrs Bull organised the cooking there were, according to two accounts, 'two wee wifies from Dundee'. Alex Ferguson remembers that, 'their cooking was more to the standard of a greasy spoon transport caff', and he remembers them, 'dishing up a breakfast of a hard boiled egg per person at the table, sunk in an ashet of baked beans and kept hot in the oven.' Rab Smith thought that they, 'produced porridge, classic fried Scots brekkies and tons of toast ... the evening meals were pretty satisfying too.'

Now we can name one of those two 'wee wifies', because a hosteller well remembers his tenth birthday, which was on 23 July 1962. His dad brought him to Braemar, and a walk through the Lairig Ghru was his birthday treat. They arrived at Loch Morlich hostel at ten o'clock at night, and they had kept his birthday cards for him, not only that, one of the cooks had baked a cake for him; that cook's name was Jeannie Grieg.

Rab Smith also remembers a visit by a group of high-ranking visitors from the middle east, who brought servants and bodyguards with them. The 'elite' of that group, used to staying in high class hotels, asked for private rooms; that, according to Rab, 'had assistant warden Dennis Fagan's eyes bulging'.

It may be that Dennis and the 'two wee wifies' did not get on well together, though. Billy MacLean remembers once seeing Dennis leave the double doors of the big fridge partly open at night, 'so that it would defrost overnight, because he didn't like the old wifies'."

"The Dundee connection was maintained with the arrival of Jim Williamson. A tall man, tartan shirted, wore glasses, and often carpet slippers in the hostel, kind eyes. Jim was quite relaxed in his role of assistant warden and would spend evenings chatting with the hostellers. He had a brother, Boyd, and I remember when he came up to stay there was some language difficulties between our Manchester familiy and Boyd's broad Dundee accent. This was at a time when Aviemore were just beginning to form an ice hockey team. Dundee has long been famous for its hockey teams, and Jim and Boyd were great supporters so they took an interest. Jim married Sue and went back with her to Dundee when he left the hostel.

Names of other assistants in those early years are just these: Jock Watt, Jean McKimmie, Edward Black, and John, his second name escapes me."

"Yes, I said "I remember an Australian girl, Sandra, who was there for a short while because she took me to the Nethybridge Games once. Dear, kind John told me he was going to take over as warden at Ferniehurst Castle, and so he did, but what became of him after that, we do not know. All we can say is that these are dear friends, who will always be remembered with great affection for the part they played in the history of this hostel."

"Jennifer Curtis arrived from Sussex on a ski course in January 1969 and became assistant in May of that year. She played tennis to a high standard. She remembers that her wages were £32 per month, (subsidised by washing sheet sleeping bags of course!), and also remembers helping Mr Utsi to lead the reindeer out into their summer pastures. Of her first ski course, she remembers that a bus driver from Boat of Garten lent her his Morris Minor on the Wednesday, and she drove up to Inverness and down the side of Loch Ness looking for the Monster. That same night, 18 January, more than a foot of snow fell and the whole ski course spent the rest of the week on the Hayfield.

She was there at the same time as Harry Jamieson, Walter Lester, Gordon Tiley and Pete Judson. Jennifer not only maintained the Dundee connection but at the same time laid claim to be the first member of the marriage club when, on 19 September 1970 she married Alex Ferguson, one of the original Dundee Committee. They married in Crawley, Jennifer's home town, though Alex proudly wore his kilt, and they live happily in Dundee to this day."

"Gaile Bryson arrived on the morning of 1 January 1966. She had travelled from Newport to Crewe and then to Aviemore by sleeper train, which had fought its way through deep snow and blizzards. She quickly found, as Robin Stephens had found a few years earlier, that most folk either had hangovers or were still partying. Certainly neither taxis nor buses were forthcoming. Gaile telephoned the hostel, and was told that Dennis had gone to help out at Reindeer House; the keeper had fallen off the little bridge into the stream. Precisely what part whisky had played in that we may never know. Anyway one of the hostellers agreed to collect her and she was given a warm welcome. She slept at first in 'C' dorm. She remembers, 'listening to the wee mousies playing hockey with bits of rubble in the ceiling above.'

Gaile settled in and moved into the right hand room down here. An invaluable help to Patricia, she was quietly content to play her part in the life of Glenmore and the mountains. In 1969, she left to become warden of Minnigaff YH for a year. She and her little dog lived in a caravan at the back of the hostel and earned the princely sum of £8 per week. She also used her feminine charms to get the hairy-legged cylsists to help her with the boiler and other heavy tasks. Gaile became a close friend of our family, and remains so to this day."

"Interesting, that both of these girl assistants, Gaile and Jennifer, still have fond memories of Patricia playing her pianola in the staff room in the afternoons."

Everyone smiled and after a short pause I continued my tale. "The early 1970's were blessed by the arrival of Margaret Hutchinson and Jenni Rollo; I remember those as golden summers. We were much the same age, and quickly became life-long friends. Jenni and I were both studying history, she at St Andrews, I at Nottingham; you may think that we were taught roughly the same things, but it was not so! Anyway, the summers of those years were times of glorious freedom and, as my memory tells me, every day was filled with sunshine."

Rosie became philosophical. "I think it must be true" she giggled, "perhaps you do only remember the sunny days. Now, was this before the hostel became a Grade 1?"

"Yes" I replied, "we closed then between 11 and 4, and because it was always sunny, the beach and the mountains became our playground. Long days led to long hill walks. When we really did get the settled spells of weather (which was not that often I suppose) the clear skies meant hot days and also brilliant star-lit nights when you would not even need a torch to find your way, and we walked the hills that way sometimes. It was not unknown to find both girls walking along the beach, scanning for lemonade bottles to return to the shop to get the deposits back, yet another tale of impoverished assistants, I suppose!. Margaret recalls the time she fell asleep on the beach, and the painful evening with Patricia gently applying calamine lotion to her sore and peeling back.

There was always a great deal of mutual affection between these girls and D and P (for that is how I shall usually refer to them). Margaret came first on a ski course in 1970, and then took a summer job at the Badenoch Hotel. She would hitch up the ski road in the afternoons, and remembers D and P offering 'tea and sympathy'. Jenni was the first in what became a long and very happy association with Buckhaven High School.

Another duty which both girls were happy to perform was taking the two golden labradors, Glen and Sally, for walks, and it was while they were there that the first (of many) litters of kittens arrived, much to the delight of all concerned. Their immediate favourite was a small ginger one, they gave him the very appropriate name of Whingey Widdle."

"Those two dogs and the many cats played a very important part in the life of this hostel" interjected Rab, "and I shall with some pride and some affection relate their story to you later, but this particular time is not really appropriate, even though Margaret and Jenni both remember them fondly."

"Quite so" I replied, "though both girls ended up with an unusual cleaning job on one particuar day. Glen and Sally both slipped their leads on a walk past Glenmore Lodge. They returned to the hostel some hours later, having discovered and presumably rolled in some discarded cooking fat! Four washes and copious amounts of washing-up liquid were needed to get them presentable again.

Jenni, to her eternal credit, would play Canasta in the evenings with D and P, Margaret always avoided doing so. But it was Dennis who took Margaret into Aviemore to buy her first pair of walking boots. Plum took time to teach her how to use a map and compass, and to pass on much advice on hill walking. Margaret remembers waiting up into the small hours one night with Patricia, awaiting the return of Dennis who had gone out on a search with the Mountain Rescue team; she also fondly remembers him taking an inordinate amount of time to do a stock-take in the office, and then discovering he was listening to the cricket.

Both girls were there when the party of Belgian hostellers decided that they would help by cleaning the dining room floor and managed to borrow a mop and bucket. They left the whole floor absolutely soaked, and it stank for days. Patricia was not amused.

But the day which will live long in the memory was when Margaret was the only assistant. The hostel was quite busy, and Dennis was using his axe to chop fairly small pieces of wood into kindling. He missed, and the axe blade went straight through the end of his finger. They could not send an ambulance, and Patricia could not drive. Margaret, who had been driving for only a month and never on her own, dauntlessly set off to take him to Raigmore, without having any idea of where to find it. Dennis had his finger swathed in tea-towels and was drifting in and out of conciousness. This, however, is a story with a happy ending, and although Dennis lost the end of his finger, he returned to the hostel within a short time; this time the ambulance brought him home. Perhaps Margaret has never really been accorded the 'true heroine' status which she so richly deserves."

"Indeed, for a humble kitchen assistant it certainly was above and beyond the call of duty" observed Chris.

"Margaret was an early member of the Loch Morlich marriage bureau, she became the wife of a true man of the mountains, Stan Franklin, he and Dennis held a very high regard for each other. They went to live in Carnoustie, and for a while Margaret worked at the University of Dundee as assistant librarian in the medical school library. Jenni returned to Fife and worked for the Libraries and Museums service, leading the Archives Team for Kirkacldy."

"Mr Morison took up his appointment as Head Forester at Queens Forest (Glenmore) in 1971. He had served as a flying officer during the war, and had much affection for the Norwegians. He was happy to oversee the commemoration of the Norwegain Stone, and also to take the bookings for the Huts as well as the campsite. He and his wife Helen lived at Mayara, behind Mikel Utsi's house, until they retired in 1979, first to Nethybridge and thence to Murrayfield, back to their Edinburgh roots. Their children were Kathleen and Alan. Alan it was who worked as Dennis's assistant, along with me, during the years 1973-4. We were both convinced that one day we were going to be famous folk guitarists, playing on stage with John James and Bert Jansch; perhaps the hostellers whom we 'entertained' did not see our future quite in those terms.

Both Alan and Kathleen remember all the cats with great affection. Alan indeed remembers everything with fondness, my uncle's long deliberate silences mid-sentence, and his discussion with Plum about the decrepit state of his walking boots to which he was enthusiastically applying dubbin. 'You might just as well dubbin your feet for all the good you're doing' said Dennis. 'Aye, that's just what I've done' replied Plum.

Alan's greatest enthusiasm, however, was reserved for Patricia's knack of making great ice cream sauces, in particular the chocolate and the butterscotch; they will remain long in his memory."

Billy and I returned to the kitchen and seated ourselves at the head of the large table, blinking at the early afternoon sunshine. This was indeed the very special place, where everyone knew that whatever happened out on the hill, or in the forests, or down on the beach during the day, they could return to here to find warmth, hospitality and security. This was what Dennis and Patricia created for their friends and family. In the rest of the hostel outside this kitchen, they created an institution, and oversaw incredible growth in the tourist industry summer and winter, and their names, as Ernie Cross well described, became a by-word for hospitality in these parts. And they could not have achieved it without assistants. But every assistant always knew that this kitchen and its table was the special place for them, and every single one of them felt welcome.

"Do you know," said Billy, laughing "I really think that is a great secret." I regarded him quizically. "Well" he explained, "in the end you simply cannot tell the story of what is just an empty building and the changes that were made to it. It must be all about the people who lived in it and worked in it, who by their very nature became part of the fabric of the building, and who, each in their own way, were special." He looked up, seeking confirmation, and I smiled encouragement at him. "That was the secret that Dennis and Patricia discovered. We, all of us, feel special that we played our part, however small, in the great story of this place, and D and P helped us to know, by allowing us to be part of the family, that we were very special indeed, each in our own different ways."

"I think you have to be right, Billy" I said. "Looking back from here I can see so many people who were and are special. The Buckhaven connection grew stronger, and Tom Somerville was the sports teacher who often came with them. His niece Lynn worked as Patricia's assistant for a while in the early 80's, together with her good friend Edmonde. Lynn was always cheerful, and we had great fun in those days; when the hostel closed for a month, Lynn was very keen to make interesting pancakes with all sorts of fillings, not all of them what you might call conventional, at least for those times!"

"Dennis over the years had two 'right hand men'. The first was Paul Richardson, a climber and caver from Yorkshire. He and his climbing partner Phil would often be seen in the hostel feeding out their climbing rope to check it, and with pitons in their back pockets. Other climbers would then stop and discuss routes with them, which pleased Dennis no end.

Many an assistant could testify to Patricia's unerring accuracy with throwing a spoon across the kitchen if you aroused her wrath; Paul held the distinction, if you can call it that, of having two spoons thrown at him at once! When Gordon came up ready to replace him, the three men found time for an epic winter walk on the hill together, very carefully using ice axes to descend an ice-laden Coire Raibert to a frozen Loch Avon and trudging back through the deep snow over the Saddle and down Strath Nethy."

"Gordon took a little time to settle in, but in the end he stayed for the greater part of the 1980's. He would make an effort to befriend the leaders of the big groups which were becoming a feature of those times. That, to some extent was forced upon him with Jimmy, the leader from Lawside Academy in Dundee. No sooner had his kids unpacked, than they all went down to Glenmore Shop and just about ransacked the place. The policeman gathered them in the common room and said that he would go for a walk, and all the sweets and stuff had better be put back on the table by the time he returned. That was partially successful, but for a day or two afterwards we would find chocolate bars and bags of sweets hidden in the most amazing places. Jimmy made sure that the next group who came behaved in a more civilised manner!

Another group of regular visitors were the British Aerospace team from Preston, who built the 'Lightning' aircraft. Gordon became a special friend to most of them, Ben and June, and Ernie Cross, who wrote the best-selling book, 'Short Walks in the Cairngorms'.

Gordon also established a good relationship with Iain Findlater, who brought many groups to Glenmore, and indeed still does.

In the winters he came to know Brian, who regularly brought his two young sons at week-ends, training them to be racers. Two people who booked on the ski course frequently during Gordon's time were Andrew Baxter from Alnwick, who most people will remember with affection, and the remarkably named Len Snowball.

He approached ski instructor Christopher Martin with some caution, but eventually began to borrow his newspaper! From there, he looked at the health foods which Christopher was fond of eating, and managed to persuade him that Guiness was indeed good for him!

It was Gordon who called my attention one day to an enthusistic skier who had not only skied back to the hostel but was even pulling himself up the steps to the front door, using his arms on the handrail, which was quite a feat of strength. He eventually took his skis off in the porch, somewhat to our relief. Dennis would often sternly remind people to remove their boots before entering the hall, we cannot dare to imagine his reaction if someone had skied up to his office! Perhaps the guy only wanted to send postcards to his friends saying that In Scotland, you can ski from the front door of your hostel!

Kitchen assistants during Gordon's time were Lynn and her friend Edmonde, then later on, dear Liz Rochester, Jenny who only stayed for a short while, and Sheila Hall.

When we closed in the autumn, as well as all the cleaning and laundry, we would also give the old homestead a new lick of paint. Duncan McKenzie was the painter who became good friends with Gordon. When we had one of the fairly major alterations done, they laid the hall floor with carpet tiles of two shades of brown. Gordon helped with much of that, and also had the idea of arranging them to form the letters 'SYHA' in front of the warden's office. He was not present, however, when a few of us were sitting in the hall and, to our absolute horror, saw one of the carpet tiles begin to move. We were still working out just how to cope with this, when the tile was pushed to one side, and a furry paw appeared, followed by the ears and then the whiskers and face of Sandy Morlich. The poor cat had been frightened by all the workmen tearing the building apart and decided to hide from it all under the floorboards."

"He had a mischievous sense of humour. For a while we put a TV in the quiet room. Gordon had the remote control in the office, but the hostellers could change channels with the buttons on the TV. Gordon worked out that if you stood to the left of the counter and reached out, you could point the remote control at the TV. Thus when someone would change a channel, Gordon would change it back again! If someone came to the office to ask what was happening he would become innocence personified and explain that we were close to high mountains and TV signals would often do strange things!

On occasions, at closing time, we would go to the common room and the members' kitchen and say that it was time for bed. We would then return to the hall, switch off the lights there, and would sit in the corner by the window. The hostellers would come, chatting in twos and threes and usually would not notice us. Just as they would climb the first stair, we would chorus 'Good Night', and we always enjoyed the startled reaction."

"When he really began to settle in he acquired a black labrador, quite appropriately called 'Bennet', who just loved to be outdoors, and lived to a good old age as well."

"Gordon was an all-round sportsman, indoor and outdoor. Winter climber, summer hill walker and he skied to instructor standard. He dutifully played Canasta, and enjoyed the Chinese version of it, Mah-Jong; whenever the dining room was empty, we would push two tables together to make a king-size table tennis table, and the ball would often spin crazily through the air at high speeds. Darts was a great love of his, and he was reckoned to be one of the best players on the 'Winky' team, even if he did sometimes need two, or three pints before he could be sure of hitting 180's."

"Gordon eventually left Loch Morlich Youth Hostel after many very happy years. He never lost touch with the outdoor sports world, though, and worked first for Graham Tiso's and latterly for Craigdon Sports. Before he left, a girl called Kate became a regular visitor to the hostel and a good friend to all of us. She enjoyed ski-ing and loved the outdoor life. Gordon made sure that he took her with him and, as they say, they lived happily ever after!"

I sighed. "And perhaps through it all, the one who oversaw so much of it was dear Carolyn Malam. She came from the railway town of Crewe, and her brother Colin and sister Cherry were frequent visitors. Carolyn made herself everybody's friend, but there was always special affection between her and D and P, and also Plum. Carolyn combined the roles of assistant and ski instructor quite effortlessly. She loved all the cats, and they certainly made it plain how much they loved her. D and P began to take regular holidays in May, confident that Carolyn would be able to handle the steadily increasing number of meals, and she went cheerfully about it all with an infectious smile. It was a delight for all of us when she married Joe Burns, himself a gifted ski teacher and cross-country man."

"In the later years, Sheila Hall came to work with us in 1982, before settling in Glasgow to pursue her musical talents and to train in travel medicine. She had a wee maroon mini, and we were often surprised how many could fit inside it to get to Aviemore.

And then came dear Mary, the Queenslander. I can just see her now, Billy, sat at that low stool, stirring her large pot of 'Soup du Jour' and explaining to all and sundry in her Aussie drawl that it was nobody's business what went into it. I remember one incident with a school group. I know that kids like tomato ketchup, but one lad on this course seemed to be a little heavy on it, even by kids' standards. One morning Mary greeted me laughing, and said I had to come and see this. The young man poured out his cornflakes into the bowl, put on the milk, and then squeezed ketchup onto it! Mary was there during the end days, when Patricia left the hostel in 1990."

We nodded to each other and smiled. "All these," said Billy as he put his arm round me, "all of these we will remember with affection in our hearts."

The Bus Drivers; Their Story

We had no sooner reached the staff room where the guests were waiting and chatting than there was a loud knock upon the kitchen door. I went to open it and two smiling faces were looking at me through the glass. Two gentlemen came in, one with a beard, and each of them very smartly dressed in the uniform of the Highland Omnibus. We greeted each other warmly and they sat down at the kitchen table. "Thank you for inviting us to this great feast John, we have come to tell you our story of how we transported people up and down the Cairngorm ski road, and in all sorts of weather conditions too. It is a great story which needs to be told, of the people and the buses involved at the time of the great explosion of interest in this area, both in summer and winter, something which we all experienced together. We are, I think with some justifcation, proud of the part which we played in it."

"Dear Raymond and Iain" I replied, "you are as welcome now as you always were. I feel obliged to offer some light refreshment before dinner, but knowing that you are seated where most of your colleagues sat on those winter mornings, perhaps I should offer you bacon rolls!"

Raymond laughed, "Indeed," he said "sometimes drivers would come back and tell us what they had to eat, and sometimes they even said it was their main meal of the day! But I like to think that most of us knew how to behave ourselves, and we learnt to do as we were told. If some toast was spare, or if indeed they were making one bacon roll and offered to make another one, then that is what we had. It is important to let you know that each and everyone of us was grateful for our breakfast, whatever form it took."

"And in turn I can say" I said, "that Patricia and all her assistants, however busy they were at that time in the morning, always took pleasure in being able to feed you, as a way of thanking you for the good service which you always offered to us."

Iain smiled. "Well, you have invited us to a feast, so we thought that the best way to begin our story would be to tell you about another feast which took place long ago. This one was in December 1966, and was held at the Palace Hotel in Grantown, which is now the Grand View Nursing Home. More than 40 people were there, in kilts and evening dresses. The occasion was a farewell dinner for Norman Smith, prior to his bus service routes being taken over by the Highland Omnibus. Norman was very much a business-man, and his business was motor transport of every kind.

He had a shop in Forest Road, Grantown, on the site where the telephone exchange is now, which advertised the AA, Esso and Leyland cars. From there he hired out cars, serviced cars and ran a taxi service."

It was Raymond who took up the story. "Well, they do say that it is an ill wind which blows nobody any good; when the forever infamous Dr Beeching closed down the local railway routes here, which people relied upon, Norman Smith saw that as a business opportunity and he began to build up a fleet of buses, mostly Bedfords, to supply those routes. Locally, he acquired the school contracts, and then ran bus services from Grantown to Forres, Elgin and Kingussie. Glenmore was not high on his agenda at first, his buses ran up that road on Wednesdays, Saturdays and Sundays, for July and August only."

Iain smiled. "But then he encountered the huge rise of interest in ski-ing, and poor old Norman was not best equipped to cope with it. Some people remember those old Bedford VAS's breaking down, and with water and brake fluid pouring out of the bonnets, but if you consider what they were expected to do, it was remarkable. First they had to negotiate the famous 'zig-zags' up the steepest section of the ski road, and the first turn of that section was a very tight angle indeed. Not only that, but remember that they built the Chairlift top section first; until they completed it, Smiths Buses, having reached the car park, then had to provide a shuttle bus which wound its way up the rough track to the Sheiling, and we all know how steep that is at the top end. At least Highland never had to take that on!"

"No" replied Raymond, "Thank goodness for that, those zig-zags were quite enough to cope with, both driving up them and on the way down. Anyway, more of that later." He smiled and had another drink of coffee. "Norman at first put in what was probably a token objection to the Highland take-over of his bus routes. In September 1966 the Traffic Commissioners in Inverness informed him that the buses really needed to be made warmer, and also needed facilities for carrying skis. He decided then to allow us to take over his bus routes, and bought a garage in Grantown instead, rather than retire. His grand farewell dinner was in December of 1966, and in January 1967 the Chairman of those Inverness Traffic Commissioners, LA Wells officially approved the takeover of routes. Norman Sutherland, the General Manager of Highland Omnibus said that thery had already begun to operate services under a preliminary licence, and Mr Wells replied that Highland would be expected to operate a service between Aviemore railway station and the Coylumbridge Hotel. He went on to mention that the Coylumbridge had been operating an 'illegal' minibus service, and that he would be grateful if the Highland would take that over."

"Well, it was not deliberately illegal" replied Iain, "and the Coylumbridge were by no means the only ones operating services, it was simply a matter of supply and demand. To give examples, Frasers Coaches of Forres and Elgin were taking customers up the ski road. Those buses looked smart in their blue and cream livery - their wedding bus was purple -, and Mains of Buckie ran ski buses also."

We sat back in our chairs and relaxed, just as two bacon rolls arrived. Both bus drivers laughed out loud. "This is really for old time's sake" said Iain as they both tucked in. Raymond took up the tale again, between mouthfuls. "So that" he said, "is the story of how the Highland Omnibus came to ply it's trade up and down the Cairngorm ski road. By 1964 the bottom section of the chairlift had been completed, so the car park was as far as we ever had to go, but the road itself was still being completed in stages as we took over."

"This is what the Forest Park Guide had to say about it originally" said Iain: '

'This fine new ski road, built in 1959 by the Inverness-shire County Council, climbs to a height of 2,000 feet and gives access from Glenmore Lodge to the ski-ing grounds on the northern flanks of Cairngorm. The road climbs steadily through the pinewoods, then out into the open braes in a series of hairpin bends. There is a car park and a turning point at the top.' And it was Murray Scott himself who added: 'At Loch Morlich Youth Hostel the new ski road branches off into the hills, terminating short of Jean's Hut in Coire Cas'."

"That is what I meant," said Raymond "so whilst the Palace Hotel was busy preparing Norman Smith's farewell dinner, the 'Strathy' was able to keep us informed about two road imrovement schemes. 'The road from Coylumbridge to Coire Cas will be 18 feet wide and will be ready for the 1967-8 ski season...a further scheme from Aviemore to Coylumbridge will follow...For this winter the work as far as Glenmore Lodge is being organised to minimise interference with traffic, work from Glenmore Lodge to Coire Cas has only just started.' and by late November: 'The Cairngorm access road from the head of Loch Morlich in Glenmore to the chairlift car park is to be improved at a cost of more than £140,000. This is in order to ease the snow clearing difficulties experienced since the three-and-a-half mile road was built in 1960, and to cope with the rapid increase in traffic'. They also told us that the Allt Mhor bridge was to be widened."

"So is that when they by-passed the zig-zags?" I asked. "Certainly," replied Iain "but I seriously have to question their ability to learn from experience, as they put it." "Why is that?" I asked.

"Well, to bypass the hairpin bends they first took the road out to the east, towards Coire na Ciste. But when they brought it back again, to go over the shoulder of Cairngorm it took them through an area which all locals knew as 'the sugar bowl' and with good reason, it was a huge snow-holding area of the mountain, and the new road went straight through the middle of it. It has been tackled by ploughs ever since, and just about every one of the drivers could tell you a story about getting up that particular section of road. Raymond MacDonald's story is typical. The plough had cleared the road that morning, cutting out a bank of snow which was considerably higher than the bus. The wind, the ever-present Cairngorm wind was blowing snow off the top of that bank across the road and onto the windscreen of the bus. Raymond was using the bank of snow to his left as the only guide he had to be sure he was still on the road, and was understandably driving very slowly indeed. For a few seconds, the wind stopped, and the road ahead became visible. Just a few feet ahead of him, Raymond saw a car which had skidded and was sideways across the road in front of him, whereupon he brought the bus safely to a stop."

The bacon rolls were finished, enjoyed, appreciated. "Well" said Iain, "they continued to improve the road and by the early 1970's they had extended it to Coire na Ciste and built a large car park there as well. I am sure there are more terrifying tales of ascents and descents of that road, but we will save those for later. Perhaps we ought to tell you something about the buses that we drove. The growth of the tourist industry was shadowed to a large extent by major changes and expansion in the transport sector. Ribble Motors of Leyland near Preston were expanding at this time, as were Alexanders of Falkirk. In 1971 we ourselves took over MacBraynes bus routes, and it is by no means irrelevant that, 6 years earlier, the City of Glasgow decided to replace its trolley buses, and the first fleet of motor buses was deemed to be unsuitable, perhaps because of narrow doors. We acquired some of those, and I remember that only one person at a time could enter, not good when we were really busy. So coach bodies and chassis were being transferred around the country. We had two large bus workshops in Inverness, both in Seafield Road, and they would do alterations as we required them.

The first problem that we addressed, as indeed we were obliged to do, was to increase our capacity for carrying skis. For that purpose, from the mid 1960's to the early 70's, we acquired buses from Ribble Motors, and Seafield Road fitted them with ski racks on the back."

Raymond laughed. "That was not a system which lasted very long. Some drivers can remember being at the meeting when we decided to scrap them. It was because too many people were hitching a ride on them!"

"Aye, well!" said Iain, "so instead we took some of the 45-seaters and removed three pairs of double seats at the front to make way for an inside ski rack. To compensate, we added a couple of triple seats in front of the bench seat at the back. That is the system that you would have been most familiar with, John."

"Yes" I replied, "that worked fine for some years, until our numbers on the ski courses grew so much that you provided double-deckers for us at the busiest times."

"Well, just briefly to complete the story for you, there was a general replacement of buses from 1972-3 until the 1980's; they were predominantly Fords, with bodywork by Willow Brook or

Alexanders. A second general replacement followed in the 1980's, and that is when the double deckers came in. The blue ones would have been Leyland Olympians - generally known as Titans, and the red ones were Daimler Fleetliners. They were certainly needed when you had 70 or more on your ski courses."

"So, please tell us about your dealings with the hostel itself then, because it became such a close relationship over the years, there remains much respect and affection between us" I said.

"It was a contract between Highland Omnibus and SYHA" said Raymond, "mostly in winter, occasionally in summer. We would collect whoever needed from the Saturday evening train, and if there were sufficient numbers, return them to Aviemore railway station the next Saturday. We had two depots, Grantown and Aviemore. It was mainly the Grantown boys who did your run Monday to Friday. Until the mid 80's, they would begin by picking up all the Chairlft staff from wherever they lived, Nethybridge, Aviemore or wherever. Having delivered them up the hill, they would come back to the hostel. Coming that way, though, the turn up to the hostel drive was very tight, until they widened it; even then we sometimes had to drive in, reverse and then we were able to get up the drive. After we had delivered the ski course, and the instructors up the hill, we had a 10.20 service bus to do. That worked fine most days, but when the whole road was one big traffic jam because of the snow we had to use a reserve driver for the service bus, and we would often be in the same queue together."

"Many was the day when the weather would disrupt normal operations" I said, "I know that, whenever he could Plum would keep the ski course down at Glenmore and take them on the Hayfield, or up the forestry tracks behind the hostel, or on wild adventures through the forest onto the beach, when we all came back covered in snow. The gradual advent of cross-country skis made that sort of operation much easier. But when the wind made ski-ing just impossible, you would take us to the Lecht, or to Slochd where we skied a few times in the fields up there, or when everywhere was stormbound you might take us to a distillery. How did that work, then?"

"Oh, it was all negotiated between Highland management and SYHA" said Raymond, "but to be honest, we all quite enjoyed a day out."

"Well, instructors and hostellers certainly appreciated it" I said. "When we toured the distillery and all (sometimes) got a wee free sample, what did you get out of it?"

"Some places treated us better than others" said Raymond, "at the distillery we put one tick against our name in a book. At the end of the season, however many ticks you had, decided the size of the bottle you might get to take home!"

I smiled at my two guests. "I feel bound to ask you," I said "what about your uniforms for Highland Omnibus?"

Iain smiled in return. "Drivers' jacket was dark blue, so dark it was almost black, same for the trousers - always smartly pressed of course. Blue shirt and tie, and caps were optional. The blue V-neck sweaters we all liked wearing were not free; we paid a subsidised price for them, I think £2 and they had the Highland Omnibus name stitched into them. We wore our licence number on the left side, a round white badge with a red circle round the outside. Most Highland drivers were prefixed 'LL' and a 5 digit number. Jack Burgess, who worked for Norman Smith, had only 3 digits on his badge!"

Raymond had decided that it was high time that we started telling some good stories. "Our buses all had twin wheels at the back," he said "and Seafield Road tried their best to help us, cross-cutting the tyres, and gradually replacing the vacuum brakes with air-assisted brakes. It really did help, but there were some times when the extremes of weather caused problems.

They had one solution which they used sometimes when the road was a mass of snow and ice: they would stop all the cars at the Hayfield, but of course we had to drive the shuttle buses up. One particular day, Jack Burgess had managed to drive as far as the last straight section before the car park before his wheels started to slip. Unobserved by Jack because of the wild weather, the Police landrover was following him. On seeing the bus begin to slide, the landrover reversed off the road into a cutting. Jack, intent only on bringing the bus back under control, saw the cutting and promptly reversed the bus into both the cutting and the Police landrover! 'I hope to goodness you're insured' was all the policeman was reported to have said. Jack's comments are not available."

It was my turn for a story. "I was with Iain Rose one day when we got as far as the cattle grid, quite a steep section of the road. He asked us all to go to the back to help him get traction. The car in front had no such advantage and slowly skidded to a stop. Iain kept the bus moving very gently forwards, and pushed the car onwards and upwards until the driver could make his own way forwards again. The driver was grateful to Iain, who explained that if he had stopped then the whole road would have come to a standstill."

"Coming down could be equally adventurous! One evening, in the gathering gloom, Raymond MacDonald found himself in the middle of a long line of traffic making its way very gingerly down the ski road which was little better than a sheet of ice. Raymond slotted the bus into its lowest gear, and realised that if he so much as touched the brakes the bus would skid sideways. The only trouble was, he was travelling about two miles an hour faster than the cars in front of him. He pulled out onto the other side of the road and, thankfully after a few minutes, was able to identify a section of road where it was safe to bring the bus to a stop. Just what the car drivers must have thought when they saw the bus overtaking them we will never know!"

Iain's grin was nothing if not mischievous. "Many a ski instructor can tell stories about those zig-zags, how you were often required to get out and push to help the bus around those tight corners. And many, probably including yourself John can tell of when the instructors had to push us up the last slope before the car park, and you will remember the driver's grin as he shouted to you 'Thank you, but I dare not stop now'. I daresay the walk did you all a power of good and warmed you up nicely for ski-ing!"

"It certainly did" I replied, "and in return I can tell you a 'Plum' story about the bus. This was a day when the wind was really blowing a hoolie, and yet the school group seemed reluctant to give up the idea of ski-ing for the day. In the way that Plum had, he agreed to take them up the hill anyway, 'just to show them what it was like'. When they arrived at the Ciste car park, the wind was buffeting the bus itself, but the teacher of the group was still not discouraged. Plum had a quiet word in the driver's ear - it was John Duncan- and said, 'just park the bus facing the wind, would you'. John duly obliged and the teacher requested that they should at least get out of the bus. When John opened the door, one little boy was quicker than everyone else in his eagerness to get outside. It is a good thing that he first held on to the pole in the middle of the door, because the wind lifted him off his feet and the little lad found himself nearly horizontal hanging for dear life onto the pole. The boy came to no harm, ski-ing was abandoned for the day, and Plum no doubt puffed contentedly on his pipe."

We all chuckled at that. Iain spoke next. "The last story that we shall tell you before we join the others does not involve the ski road at all, it is simply about a gentleman for whom we feel sorry. This took place on a cold and dark January Saturday night. It was the turn of Raymond MacDonald to meet the London train and take any ski course members up to the hostel. Raymond dutifully brought the bus smack on time at 7.30 to Aviemore railway station; there he found a young gentleman waiting for him who had got off an earlier train from Glasgow. 'Is this the bus for Loch Morlich Hostel?' 'Yes it is, please get on and keep yourself warm, I will go and collect the others from the London train.'

Raymond walked into the station to be told that the train would be perhaps half an hour late. Half an hour passed, the night grew a little darker and a little colder. Raymond returned, and was informed again that the train might be half an hour. On his third enquiry he was informed that the train had left Perth and would be here in due course. Eventually, at nearly eleven o' clock the train arrived, and six people alighted. 'Are you for the ski course at Loch Morlich Hostel?' Raymond asked them. 'Oh, no, we have just arrived on holiday and we are staying at the Cairngorm Hotel just over the road there.' The poor gentleman from Glasgow was given a late and lonely supper at the hostel!"

"So that" explained Iain, "completes our story of the contract between SYHA and the Highland Omnibus!" He raised his eyebrows. "It certainly does not complete the story at all" I said, "it would mean nothing if we did not remember the drivers of all these buses who made it all possible."

Raymond laughed. "That is quite true, John" he said, "I shall tell that part of the great story. "There was quite an overlap between Smith's buses and the Highland. The drivers who worked for both were Iain Rose, John Watson, Norman Holmes, Archie Little, Jack Burgess, Kenny Aberdeen, and Jimmy MacDonald who went on to work for the ambulances. There was also Malcolm Vaughan who lived in Boat of Garten. There were also two who had earlier worked for Alexanders."

"Who were Alexanders?" I asked. "Alexanders of Falkirk" smiled Raymond, "were a small company who grew to be big. They started bus routes locally, but then had to split into three groups in the early 1960's. By the 1980's they had become one of the largest suppliers of double-decker buses in the world, and also built DMU carriages for British Rail. Their three bus groups were Fife, Midland Scottish and Northern Scottish; it was Northern Scottish who employed Jock Grant and John Duncan before they came to Highland. Alexanders eventually became Bluebird."

"Anyway" Raymond continued, "we had two depots to supply the local routes: Grantown and Aviemore. It would have been mostly the Grantown boys who drove the ski road buses, but not exclusively so. Based at Grantown were Jack Burgess, Jock Grant, John Duncan who, like John Garrow would sometimes go ski-ing if he had an hour or so before his next service; there were also Andy Murray, Alasdair Little, Michael George, Iain Chason, and Angus Shearer, who passed his bus-driving test and got his badge on 17 November 1977, the same day as Raymond MacDonald. Andy Murray enjoyed life with a smile on his face; the other drivers would gather around Andy to hear the funny story of the day.

From the Aviemore depot came Alan Greenyear, Iain Rose, Raymond MacDonald, John Watson, Roy Lambeth (widely known as 'Roy the Boy'), George Cameron, Fergie Smith the photographer, Jimmy Powell, and dear Robert Drummond. Like Andy Murray, Robert was never lost for a good story or the latest joke. When he drove the hostellers down to the Coylumbridge for swimming or skating, everybody laughed all the way there and all the way back. Robert went on to drive the inter-city buses and to become an Inspector, but always kept the same mischievous smile on his face."

"My own memory is a little confused with the 'Malcolms'," I said. "Of course I remember Malcolm Vaughan, he was based at the Grantown depot and was a friend of D and P; there was a Malcolm who was a request driver for the London Ski Club, and would bring them either to Aviemore or the Craiglynne Hotel. It was also a Malcolm who brought the Edinburgh Ski Club to Cairngorm, 'who always got us there on those evening journeys through drifts and moonlit ice', as some of them remembered. I do not suppose they could all have been the same person, perhaps Malcolm was just a popular name for bus drivers!"

I smiled at both gentlemen. "So now your story is complete" I said, "Thank you for telling it to us, please join the other guests getting ready for the great feast we will serve to you shortly; and once more we thank you for the wonderful service all your drivers gave to us, and know that we always did and always will hold you in great affection and friendship."

"And thank you, good Sir" said Iain, "we were proud of the part we played in your great story, and we will always be grateful to your uncle and aunt, and of course the assistants who fed us and looked after us so well."

The Wardens; their Tale

I followed the bus drivers into the staff room where all the guests were now seated. I smiled as I prepared to address them, and my smile was returned by all. "I want to thank you all for coming today" I began, "and especially for telling us such wonderful stories. However, as the great feast is not quite prepared yet, I think it is time for me to take my turn in telling you all a tale. This is the story of how my auntie and uncle came to take over this Youth Hostel, and how they guided it and cared for it for all those magical years, when people would ski well into the month of May, and when long summer days drifted into evenings where the twilight would last until dawn, when the sun rose over Ryvoan Pass."

There were nods of general agreement. "Are you sitting comfortably?" I began.

"Dennis was my father's brother. He came from the north side of the City of Manchester, in Chadderton, and was an accountant for the great cotton mills which had brought Manchester its fortune. He had a mathematical brain, which made the adding-up of Youth Hostel register pages easy for him, and also made him a formidable chess player. He brought to the hostel with him one of the old ledgers he used to work with, a great, tightly bound black book with dozens of columns on each page, pounds, shillings and pence printed at the top. The hostel register pages were in the same format at first, and I have seen my uncle draw three fingers slowly down each of the three columns and then simply write in the total at the bottom!

His ability to understand a pack of cards came from his father, my grandfather whom I met only for the briefest of times. He was a professional gambler who kept the family mainly by playing solo whist; Dennis preferred Canasta.

His greatest love, though, was rock-climbing. He had a climbing partner, Bob, who eventually went to live in Australia. Every available week-end the two companions would ride their motor cycles from Manchester to North Wales, and take on the great crags of the Snowdon Horse-shoe."

I smiled. "I fondly remember one magical half-term holiday from school in Manchester. Dennis came down to collect me and took me to the youth hostels of Snowdon Ranger, Bryn Gwynant and Idwal Cottage. His picture was on the wall of the dining room at Idwal Cottage."

"Meanwhile, in a house in Audenshaw, there lived three sisters. The youngest was Patricia, and she was born and went to school in Canada, in a town called Lloydminster, which straddles the border between the states of Alberta and Saskatchewan. She held a Canadian passport."

"Having got married, off they set on the great adventure of their lives together. They arrived in a splendid grey Humber Hawk, with a column gear-change and a bench front seat. That car would have dropped a gear to climb up Shap Fell (before they built the M6) and it would have wound its way through the narrow roads leading to Crieff; they would have stopped in the little car park by the river at the Sma' Glen. They would have called in at the magical little tea room in Dunkeld for bacon rolls or Walkers shortbread, and delicious coffee. Arriving at Aviemore they would have driven past the Pot Luck Tea Rooms and the Co-op. Then they would have turned right and followed a narrow road which plunged downhill and swung left to take them under the railway. Right again, past three low cottages, and then left to cross the River Spey. That old metal bridge was 'Constructed by the Tees-Side Iron and Engine Works Co. Ltd. Engineers. Middlesbro'-on-Tees' and it was only just wide enough for that old grey Humber Hawk. They would have driven past the school and village green at Rothiemurchus, and on to Coylumbridge, with its little gift shop. Thereafter they would have followed a single-track road with a few passing-places, over the cattle grid just before the trees cleared and offered them the stunning view over Loch Morlich to the northern corries of the Cairngorm Mountains. Coming to Glenmore they would have turned left by Sandy's Shop and followed a Forestry track up to the hostel which was to become their home.

Timmy the black cat accompanied them on that first journey, who discovered on his arrival that a large grey-striped cat was already in residence there. Sandy Morlich had somewhere lost half of his tail, and his general appearance, together with his flat ears meant that he was often mistaken for a wildcat. Perhaps the most remarkable thing about him was that he would cheerfully eat slices of cucumber!

Dennis would no doubt have been delighted to come to a place which is a paradise for climbers in summer and winter. But as a young married couple it must have been a difficult decision to give up a salary and to take over a new hostel which had previously seen only a succession of temporary wardens. As Dennis began to extend the hand of welcome to the walkers and climbers, so they responded by returning to the hostel in steadily growing numbers. All of this, of course, took time, and that time was exactly what Patricia needed to find her feet and to come to terms with the many needs of catering, in which she had no previous experience. Bella brought the milk from Homelands Dairy; Walkers provided all the bread, white and brown sliced loaves and many rolls. Eggs were supplied by Mr Gammie. Meat and almost everything else came from local suppliers whenever she could find them.

And then their daughter Ruth was born, and went to school in Rothiemurchus. Patricia's sister Winnie Kenyon had children, Alan, Joyce and Barbara and they spent many school holidays here. The local children were two girls, Maria Matlack and Anne Cameron."

I smiled at my audience. "As for me, well, I negotiated with my parents in Manchester and reluctantly agreed to spend a few days here one summer. I stayed for the whole of the school summer holidays. That Christmas, one of my presents was from Dennis and Patricia. It was a Silva compass, and the card said: 'To help you to find your way north.' It was at that moment that I knew that I had to follow them and make my life in this beautiful place also."

"So that is how the younger generation came to Glenmore. But we must return to our story of the pioneers themselves."

"They settled in to the flat at the top of the stairs. It had a bedroom, a sitting room and a bathroom. Dennis brought with him a black and white TV, mainly to watch cricket. Reception was almost non-existent, except when weather conditions in the northern corries were just right and the wind was in the right direction, when he could watch some very crackly ITV programmes. The BBC contacted him and politely requested a licence fee. Dennis pointed out that as he could not get any of BBC's programmes, he had no intention of paying them a licence fee. The arguement went on for several years before he bowed to the inevitable rule of law; but he had made his point."

"As Patricia was sorting out how to feed everybody, Dennis settled into his office, which was where the Quiet Room is now. As it grew steadily busier, so he began to stock the shelves with tinned goods, drinks, and chocolate bars, giving pride of place to his favourite Cadbury's fruit and nut bars. 'The best food to take on the hill with you' he would often exclaim. He also stocked SYHA's range of handbooks and maps, badges, of cloth and of metal, including the 'Highlander' and the 'Saltire', 'Contour' road books, international song books, and post cards of the hostel which always sold well. Once a month, of course, he had to send accounts to head office. That was to Dundee at first, because the hostel was listed as L5 in Dundee district. Eventually things became centralised at 7

Glebe Crescent Stirling FK8 2JA. At the end of every month a large brown envelope was dispatched thither, containing all the register pages (added up correctly), all the 'C' cards, (advance bookings) together with a monthly accounts sheet which listed every item stocked and which must of course balance with the money banked. Dennis always achieved this with great ease; one assistant remembers that on one occasion, he seemed to be taking much longer than usual to balance the books. On closer investigation she discovered that the radio was on, and the third Test between England and Australia was at a critical stage."

It was one of the ski-instructors who spoke up. "There must be lovely memories for you of those early years and the long summer holidays from school."

I smiled wistfully. "They always told me that the first walk they ever did together, having arrived at the hostel, was to the Green Loch in Ryvoan Pass. And the best times for us younger ones were on brilliant summer mornings with Patricia. She would find some empty Jam tins - the large catering ones - she would make holes in the top and attach some string. With these around our necks we would set off up the track to Badaguish and collect as many raspberries and blaeberries as we could fit into those tins. Of course our red-stained fingers and mouths told the story of how many berries did not find their way to the tin! We would usually sing as we were walking, 'Step we Gaily on we Go' was a favourite; and the pies which followed our berrying expeditions were delicious."

"Yes," said Rab "but surely, once your aunt and uncle were settled in and had put the hostel onto an even keel, didn't that co-incide with the huge growth in the ski tourism industry?"

Oh, certainly" I replied, "winter courses were always a priority for SYHA, and they set up an office in Edinburgh specially to deal with them. You might well say that the final piece of the jigsaw of the great success that the ski courses became was when Plum arrived as Chief Instructor. Like Dennis, he came from a Manchester mountaineering background; right from the start and throughout their professional lives together there was much mutual respect between those gentlemen."

"It was the success of the ski courses which prompted much discussion between Dennis and National Office. Why could we not offer summer courses run along the same lines? Out of that came the 'Try a Sport' courses which ran for six summers. They were broadly run on the same lines as the ski courses, all meals and packed lunches were included, but we never used our own instructors. The hill and forest walking was looked after by Iain Hudson of Highland Guides at Rothiemurchus; the watersports were contracted to Cairdsport, David Barclay and Derek Brightman. I Like to think that if they had taken off we would have used our own instructors just like the ski school, but the truth was that, although a few people booked every week, the numbers never looked likely to match the ski courses. That said, everyone who came on those courses had a thoroughly enjoyable time, we heard some hair-raising tales about the last day canoe trip down the river Spey, and some became great friends, and returned in the winter.

It was precisely to that end that D and P began to build up a slideshow. Patricia took some quite stunning pictures of the local wildlife, and Dennis took the camera on his expeditions to the high tops of the Cairngorms, including his favourite walk down Coire Raibert to Loch Avon. When the slides were sufficient to fill two magazines, it became a tradition to show it in the dining room on a Tuesday evening, summer and winter. The summer visitors in particular always expressed surprise at the sheer volume of snow on the mountains, and a few skiers returned to walk the summer pathways. We always finished the slide show with some quite spectacular shots of sunrise over Cairngorm, the northern lights, and pink shimmering evening skies."

"Whenever the weather was particularly inclement, and whenever we had school parties in who were perhaps not adequately equipped with outdoor clothing, Dennis would use some of the slides to illustrate his point about safety on mountains, a subject which was dear to his heart. 'It is no use at all having a map and compass if you do not know how to use them!' he could often be heard to exclaim. He had concern for the safety of everyone who came to his hostel, and was acutely aware of its remote position. At the busiest times he might tell someone who had arrived by car that we were full that night, in order to keep two beds free for folk who might have walked there over the mountains.

The warden at Braemar was a remarkable lady called Marie Ewan. She and Dennis kept in close touch by telephone every summer, telling each other each day just how many folk had left their hostel to walk through the Lairig Ghru. On a shelf in the hall there was a log book. A hardback A4 lined ledger, the first one was red and the second black. Inside that book everybody, as a matter of course would write their name, the number in their party, their intended route and an alternative if possible, and their estimated time of arrival. It seems not to be fashionable to do that nowadays, but for many years people were happy to use it, we checked every evening to see if anyone had not returned, and it gave a good excuse for folk to tell us stories of their day 'on the hill.'

Sometimes it did not go according to plan. In September 1965 Andrew Bluefield set out from the hostel to Ben Macdui. He became dis-orientated in the swirling misty weather and was lost on the mountain for two days. The next year a young gentleman from Wiltshire set off to go climbing. He was caught out by a sudden change in the weather and by the early onset of darkness. Dennis raised the alarm when he did not return and a full scale search was made for him on Saturday night. Thankfully, Robert walked back to the hostel unaided on Sunday morning, after an unpleasant night on the hill.

Molly and Joe Porter were the mainstays of the Cairngorms Mountain Rescue Team at this stage, and they lived in the Sheiling for a while as wardens. New Year was and is always the busiest time for the Rescue Team. In 1967/8 a party of three attempted what was described as 'an adventurous crossing of the Lairig Ghru' in horrendous conditions of deep snow and avalanches. Again Dennis alerted the teams when they failed to arrive, and again, thankfully, they returned under their own steam, after a very cold overnight bivouac. In January 1968 there was a large avalanche in Coire Raibert. Dennis helped to organise a search to find three lads from Edinburgh who had been forced to stay out overnight when one of them was injured by the avalanche.

One summer, two folk from the campsite set off to climb Bynack More intending to return over the Saddle. They had used our log-book. One injured his leg on the rocks, and after spending two nights out in the open they arrived at Tomintoul!

Sadly, you did not always have to go onto the mountains to get into serious trouble. In August 1965 an 18 year old man drowned in the cold waters of Loch Morlich; he was only 30 yards out from the shore. The loch is a kettlehole, it has a shelf near the shore and then drops steeply down to about 40 feet.

That contrasts with a story that Dennis used to tell often, of a guy who rushed into the hostel looking quite distressed. He had got his car stuck on the beach. Dennis offered to organise a group of hostellers to pull it off for him, but the gentleman still looked very concerned and asked what time the tide came in?"

Rab laughed and then looked rather thoughtful. "I rather think" he began hesitantly, "that some of us ski instructors might have been responsible for a somewhat eventful night in the history of this hostel. It was all to do with leaving jackets to dry overnight in the ski room!"

"Yes" I replied, "a night never to be forgotten. Snow had fallen, snow on snow, and I had come up for the school half-term holidays with Alan. In the middle of the night Alan shook me awake with the words, 'Get up John, there's a fire'. I leapt off the top bunk so fast I landed on one of my boots, but I did not have time to think how much that hurt. I became aware of excited voices and people running. When I looked from the window I saw to my horror that the ski room was ablaze. I have always assumed that someone had already called for the Fire Brigade, but they seemed to take an eternity to arrive. Afterwards we joked that they first had to round up the horses before they could come to our rescue! Meanwhile, the hostellers had formed a chain from the ski room along the passage and outside, and were passing skis to each other. One pair was handed to me with the tips on fire! At the same time the girls ran upstairs to try and stop the flames from reaching the main building, and for a while things were quite desperate.

But plenty of people helped and soon we had mop buckets full of water at all the critical points; we even got the hose pipe working. When we had rescued all that we could from the ski room, everyone went outside to safety. Alan and I saw that two people were sitting on a large pile of soft snow. Alan pointed out to them that they were in fact on top of a large gas tank, and they moved away with some alacrity. The arrival of the Kingussie Fire Brigade was cheered by everybody. In the way that the hostel always had, things returned to normal, and Patricia somehow managed to serve breakfast to 86 people on time, at 8.30. The dining room was buzzing with excited chatter."

It was Rosie who spoke up next. "Your uncle and auntie were very fond of pets, weren't they? Dogs and cats?"

"Ah yes" I replied. "For her birthday in 1964 Ruth was presented with a golden labrador. Her name was Glen. She possessed the soft mouth that labradors do and always wanted to carry the newspaper back from Sandy's shop. I learned to do without the soggy bits when reading it! She could also carry an egg as far as you wanted, but would never put it gently down, she always dropped it. Her nickname was 'Shadow', she would follow in close attendance, at least until the stick was hurled far along the path for her. One glorious summer, when Buckhaven High School were here along with many others, Glen produced a litter, and one of my abiding memories is of eight tiny golden lab puppies, all ears and paws, tumbling and cascading down the stairs in the morning.

We had mixed feelings when the last of those puppies was given away, but a short time later, Sally was returned to us, her owner had to go back 'down south' and we decided to keep her. I took them both for long walks on the hill. One winters morning I took them to the beach and sent sticks skidding across the ice for them. Glen was a little way out; I threw a stick for Sally and she chased and then pounced on it with some force. A crack appeared and I watched amazed as it made its way unerringly towards Glen, who then disappeared with a splash. It was two very wet and cold dogs who I returned to the hostel that morning, who quickly sought out the warmest place they could find, by the ovens."

"Winter was a hard time for the cats as well. Every night they would huddle together for warmth, as close as they could get to the huge boiler which stood in a room in the back passage opposite the ski room. Every spring, the heating would suddenly go off. Dennis would phone the engineer, who would spend an hour or two cleaning and servicing that boiler, then he would cheerfully come into the kitchen for his coffee and would hand Dennis a huge ball of cat fur, and would assure him that all was well again. The only other time you could see all the cats together was when Patricia

114

would buy stewing steak. She would be seated on her stool at the large kitchen table, trimming the fat off the meat. She would then have the undivided attention of the whole family of felines, arrayed in a perfect semi-circle around her stool, eyes expectant, tails curled neatly around their front paws."

Rosie smiled. "How many were in that family, John?" she asked. I grinned. "It was not easy to be certain at any one time just how many were around. I think there might have been as many as 14 eventually; but they certainly kept the mice, voles and other small woodland creatures out of the building. Now let me see, Timmy and Sandy you already know about. I shall tell you of the others as I recall them. Big Ging(er) was a huge cat, better suited to being a back-street tom. He would roam far and wide, go missing for three or four days and would return home to be comforted with perhaps a bit of his ear and some lumps of fur missing. I hope he sorted out the opposition! We were seated at the kitchen table one snowy night, and we heard a cafuffle on the roof. We then caught a brief glimpse of Big Ginge tumbling downwards past the window as he slid off the roof and landed with a soft thud in the snow.

DC would never roam anywhere. She was very affectionate, especially to Dennis, hence her name, Dennis's Cat. DC held us all spellbound for about 20 minutes one night as we witnessed a stand-off between her and a hedgehog. The eye contact between them was like the gunfight at the OK corral.

LC stood for Little Cat, Winjy Widdle was so named because she did both, frequently. Liadh's fur was very soft, and a deep grey colour.

The most gorgeous cat I ever saw, though, was Perry. Champagne coloured? A very light and soft pinky-grey, and of course vivid pink eyes. At all times she maintained a regal bearing. Perry and LC were two who would sleep contentedly on your lap through a whole game of Canasta!

What can I say about Gerald? A big cat, certainly, but the opposite character of Big Ginge. In short, he was a wimp. Nevertheless he was still there, prowling around the boiler house when the time came for us to leave the hostel.

The final member of the four-legged family arrived when Gordon began to settle in at the hostel. He acquired a black lab to take on walks and, quite appropriately, called him Bennet!"

"From the earliest days both Dennis and Patricia took a keen interest in the wider workings of the SYHA. Whenever time allowed one or both would attend the Wardens' Conferences. The booklet produced for the SYHA's 50th anniversary in 1981 shows pictures of them at Stirling in 1966 and at Eglinton in 1972, and I know that they went to others as well."

"Ah, I have that booklet as well" said Rab. "It shows two other interesting things. It shows a rather ancient bus with lots of skiers queueing to get into it outside this hostel. The interesting thing is that the bus is at the eastern end of the building. It would be good to know if it had to negotiate that little bridge by the forestry buildings!"

Our eyes met, and we both grinned and then laughed out loud. " I know," I said "negotiating that bridge was more than Dennis could manage some nights on his way back from the Rotary! He would ask Paul or Gordon to organise a party of hostellers to push him through the snow, all the while wearing a broad grin."

"Anyway" Rab continued, "the booklet also shows HRH the Duke of Edinburgh visiting in 1956. That, of course, was when it was still Glenmore Lodge, but it clearly shows him shaking hands over the office counter, in the Quiet Room, which, as you said, is where your uncle first had his office."

"As I had started to explain" I said, "as they took a wider interest in SYHA so they began to make friends with other wardens. We were close to Aviemore, and would always help each other out if the need arose. When I first came, dear Tom Wilson was the Aviemore warden; what a kindly man he was. I think he and his wife retired to Crieff, and soon afterwards Cameron McNeish became warden. Derek and Anna were there when we left.

Dennis had much in common with Dave Gunn at Glen Nevis; they were both climbing and mountain hostels, and a life-long friendship developed between the two men. I also heard them talk in affectionate terms of Bob and Jean Crawford at Strathtummel, of Bob Hamilton at Bruntsfield, and of Bill and Peggy Duff at Eglinton.

John and Mabel Shepherd rode a tandem. They took over at Stirling, and quickly attracted other tandem tourists to their hostel. I was asked to cover for them once while they went on holiday (taking their tandem around the west coast, of course) and I noticed as soon as I got there that three tandems were in the bike shed; it must have taken the power of two pairs of legs to get up the hill to the hostel. It was the old Earl of Mar's lodging, next door to Stirling Castle. While I was there, the Ministry of Works team discovered a stone statue of a knight hidden behind the fireplace in the old great hall."

"As time went by, so some of the regular hostellers became close friends of Dennis and Patricia. Jim and Diane Smyth were such people, as was Mike McCue who brought parties up from Liverpool."

"The British Aerospace team first came up in May 1978, and every year thereafter until 1990. The harder mountain men sometimes came up in February as well; in fact the trips began after a winter week-end in Glencoe, when the decision was taken by the whole group that self-catering was not popular, and some warmer weather would be much appreciated. Thus they decided to come to the hostel in May, and looking back, it is amazing just how often the weather was idyllic for them. They enjoyed the company of the other groups who often came at that time: St Mary's, Aberdeen, Dollar Academy and George Watson's College. Patricia looked after them all with loving care and lots of good food. It was interesting to see Jimmy Chaplin's face when his St Mary's kids put a tray of bacon back to the hatch which they could not eat, and the BEA crew promtly started making sandwiches of it for their packed lunch. The school kids had not thought of that, but they learned quickly! Dear Ben Gardner and his wife June were the leaders of the party, they made a bench and a plaque out of respect for Syd Harris when he passed on, this remains at the hostel to this day. Phil Herbert lived long, and of course there was Ernie Cross, the author. They all had a close relationship with D and P, spent many happy evenings with Dennis in the 'Winky', and in later years, Ben and June would take D and P out for dinner at the end of the week. Ernie's book, 'Walks in the Cairngorms' was published by Luath Press in 1984, and in his dedication Ernie wrote this: 'For Patricia and Dennis Rosenfield, Wardens of Loch Morlich Youth Hostel, whose hospitality has become a byeword in these byeways."

"Peter and Hanna Weiser were teachers of English at the 'Anton Bruckner Gymnasium' in the town of Straubing, Bavaria. The town sits in a quite idyllic setting on the banks of the Danube; the school of course was named after the famous composer, and so all the pupils had a good grounding in music. Peter and Hanna used their local travel firm of 'Biendl Reisen' to take parties of kids on a tour of the Highlands every summer.

Peter remembers the first time they came. He and Dennis had never met, but they had exchanged booking forms and photos. Peter parked the bus a distance away from the hostel and walked up the hostel drive. He recalls, 'a small man with a pipe in his mouth came out, stretched out his hand and said "Good Afternoon, Peter" and that was the beginning of a life-long friendship.' They would sometimes take the other group leaders out to dinner in Kincraig, D and P would look after the children. They would return about 10 o'clock and then, to reward the kids they would have a pyjama party, singing their hearts out until about midnight.

The highlights for the children were the trip to Balmoral, in case they saw the Queen, the trip down Loch Ness, wide-eyed in wonder in case Nessie should appear, and of course to Loch Morlich Youth Hostel. I remember once going with them to the beach at Nairn. The kids were so excited, and almost all of them got on their mobile phones to chatter excitedly with their parents. Peter explained to me that they live in Bavaria, which is about as far away from the sea as you can get. Gordon and I always got on well with the coach drivers, even if we could not understand each other, we learnt that they usually had cases of Bavarian beer in the boot. Over the years, Peter and Hanna became close friends of the family, they still are to this day. What magical times we had with those kids. Exploring the Glenmore forest with them, they all knew how to identify the good mushrooms from the bad ones. 'Schwammerl' they called them, a Bavarian dialect word. They would pick chanterelles and cook a big pot of them with onions and cream for supper at the hostel. Evenings were a pure delight. They would gather in the common room or outside and would play whatever instruments they had brought with them, and everyone would sing. They took a keen interest in Scottish songs and would often learn to play them and write down the words. Patricia had an Autoharp, which is a German instrument, and she would play that for them, and they would respond by singing Bavarian songs, always quite beautifully. Some of the kids would occasionally bring traditional dress with them, which looked really good in a Highland setting. They were fascinated if they could hear the bagpipes played.

Once Peter and Hanna brought a group of adults for a trip up Cairngorm Mountain, so of course they called in to say Hello.

Patricia immediately invited the whole group (of 45) to tea, and by the time they returned from the mountain she had baked scones for everybody. That is what Peter means when he talks of a very special friendship, and of why Loch Morlich will always be a special place for them, and for many hundreds of kids from Straubing.

But the best time of all, by general agreement, was when, keeping it secret from the kids until they had all said their goodbyes ('Wiederschauen') and were on the coach, Peter and Hanna invited Dennis and Patricia to come back home with them. That led to a wonderful holiday for all concerned, remembered with great affection to this day."

"They always enjoyed their holidays, didn't they?" asked Rosie. "Oh, certainly" I replied, "at first they would usually go away in May - leaving assistants to enjoy what became known as 'May-Ins' - but although there were some near disasters, the hostel was usually presentable for their return! As time went by, May steadily became a much busier month, so D and P would then go somewhere in October or November. Bavaria certainly suited Dennis because of the proximity to high Alps. He had an antique-looking 'Freytag-Berndt' map of the 'Zillertaler Alpen'. Patricia of course accompanied him as they loved to go a-wandering; she took a keen interest in the flora and fauna around her.

There were trips to south Wales, and to the Isle of Arran, Glen Sannox and Glen Rosa were their favourite walks. And several times they visited Jersey and Guernsey, flying from Glasgow."

"Several hostellers were frequent visitors and over the years became special friends. Christopher Hart described the hostel as 'a very special place, and the friendship of Dennis and Patricia was a privelege and support'. In 1974, Christopher, together with Rod, Ann, Keith Deary and Angela Dutton took a Landrover on expedition in Norway. They were using touring skis, before it became popular in the Cairngorms."

"Keith Deary first visited when it was still Glenmore Lodge, and remembers Mrs Reid being the sole occupant! He remembers a succession of wardens and temporary wardens, and that Irene Bowers did not get on well with any of them! They were days when no meals were provided, and no cars were allowed at all! Captain Bull was the last warden before Dennis. Keith once borrowed Dennis's Humber Hawk and took it into Aviemore. He can still remember his feelings when he met another car coming across the old bridge, there was just not enough room for both of them. He was also there at the time of the fire, he remembers carrying the buckets!"

"Rod Barnes was a life member. He gratuated from Cambridge University in 1963 and began to discover how wonderful life in and around the Cairngorms could be. Typically, he would arrive on the overnight train at 6am in Aviemore, have a good, warming porridge breakfast in the little cafe next to the station, he would then walk up the road to the hostel and have his second breakfast there! After which he would walk up the hill to ski, and would ski back to the hostel whenever snow permitted. He soon began to bring the University Scout and Guide Club with him, and they hired skis from Rudi's shop in Kingussie before we had enough to supply them. He led those groups for many years. He would also lead the hostel New Years Eve ceilidhs, playing his guitar until 2am while everybody danced and made merry. D and P would invite him for dinner with them, either on Hogmanay or New Years Day.

He bought a pair of touring skis from Iain Hudson at Highland Guides. Just to 'break them in' he took them up onto the plateau via the shoulder of Coire an Lochain, all the way to Ben Macdui, and from there skied all the way back down to the hostel.

In 1971 the Cambridge University Scout and Guide Club invited a girl called Ann to ski with them. Ann was on her first visit, from the School of Health Visiting in Aberdeen, so she was pleased to join the group. She was also a life member, and that evening, Dennis expressed great surprise on seeing that her card had no stamps at all; he immediately pulled Rod's card out of the cubby hole and showed her pages full of stamps, (almost exclusively of Loch Morlich). To this day Ann thinks that Dennis had a sixth sense, or at least was hugely intuitive; in October of that year Rod and Ann got married. When their second son Ian was born, they invited Patricia to be godmother."

"It is of some interest" I said, "that Rod once told me that he first came shortly after D and P had arrived. There was a red-haired assistant, Irene, who had worked under previous wardens. Dennis and Irene did not get on well. Dennis also told Rod that SYHA had appointed him with a remit to bring some order to the hostel. Which may explain why I have heard rumours that it was a fairly rowdy place in the early years."

"Dennis also told Rod that he was upset by the SYHA's insistence that he should allow a 'Space Invaders' machine to be installed in the common room. That causes me some embarassment as I remember all the afternoons Paul, Gordon and I spent saving the world from outer-space invasion!"

Rab spoke up. "It was our colleague Harry Jamieson who taught Adrian and Dineke Ward to ski. Dineke told me of one fantastic day when all the cars in the hostel car-park were buried under the snow, and the snowplough from the hill had got stuck the day before and still could not move. They heard on the radio that the train might get to Aviemore, and Dineke had to travel. So, undaunted as all of Harry's pupils were, she set off to ski to Aviemore, the only person to attempt the journey that day! On the way she approached what looked like a small crevasse, and she skied over the top of an abandoned landrover. When she finally got on the train, she told me that everyone was packed like sardines as they travelled south!"

"Yes" I replied, "she first came with her brother David, and they woud climb everything in sight, riding up the old zig-zags on the ski road on their motor scooters. They were there before Dennis came, and the wardens were temporary. Her brother John came to work for Mikel Utsi with the reindeer for a while.

She met Adrian at the hostel, and they were married in March 1972. They remain good friends with Rod and Ann, with Keith Deary and Angela Dutton, and with Julie Keenan. Dennis and Patricia became godparents to their eldest daughter, Jennifer.

They spent a couple of Hogmanays with Dave Gunn at Glen Nevis and could not help but notice the concern expressed by both wardens (and by Patricia) for their less-experienced fellow wardens. They all worked together for quite a while, Dennis asked Adrian if he would help them in his legal capacity, and in 1973 they produced a document to set up an official Wardens' Association, 'To consider all aspects of Wardens' employment, and to negotiate on their behalf'. Adrian was presented with a carriage clock at a special lunch with the Wardens' Association committee, thanking him for his contribution.

They were also well aware of just how deeply Dennis cared about the safety of all his guests, especially on the mountains. This of course is what led him to put the log book out in the hall. If time allowed he would always quiz new arrivals about their intended walks, their equipment and their experience. This happened to Adrian's sister Viv when she arrived for her first visit, but when she informed him who her brother was, he treated that answer as sufficient! Viv met her husband Dave at the hostel, thus becoming yet another member of the Loch Morlich marriage bureau!

Dennis would also use the slide show to put over his point about mountain safety, sometimes banging his knuckles on the table, saying, 'and when we eventually found him he was as frozen as this!'; on one memorable occasion he passed round a badly worn (and inadequate) shoe; as some blase person was holding it, Dennis would mention that it came off a dead body on the hill!

Best of all, though, they remember Dennis's style of wardenship, how he would use his 'sixth sense' to identify possible trouble-makers and would be vigilant in nipping trouble in the bud. And of course", here I smiled, "they like me can picture him sallying purposefully forth into the hostel with unlit pipe in his mouth, which signified that some trouble was about to be sorted out! 'Conscious and high quality, but deliberately low-key' was how Dineke described Dennis's style of wardenship. He would not always give out hostel duties to his 'usual crowd' as he did the other hostellers; but he knew at the same time that he could depend on them for the real help he needed in the hostel; how they would thaw out the members kitchen if it froze during the night, and would always check that it was acceptably clean before they went out for the day. This mutual trust always worked well, and that is why Rod and Ann, Adrian and Dineke to this day feel that they were part of Dennis and Patricia's 'extended family'; if you will, those who would come in by the back door to the kitchen, rather than through the front door."

I walked to that kitchen door thoughtfully, remembering all the cheery faces who had walked through it over all the years.

Then I returned to address my Norwegian guests, and they stood up respectfully. "I have something of interest to tell you about my friend Adrian" I said. "As he gained more experience of Cairngorms ski-ing conditions, he began to lead groups ski-touring in Norway. There he made friends with a gentleman who was still ski-ing even though he was in his ninties. He told Adrian that he camped and trained in Glen Feshie during the war years; how he gave instruction in winter warfare in Iceland. But this is really what

I want to tell you: He said that he participated in a deception that the D Day landings would take place in Norway!" The Norwegians exchanged knowing glances, and they thanked me with nods and smiles.

I looked at at all my guests. "We are coming towards the end of my tale of my uncle and aunt. Years passed, and anniversaries came along, 20, then 25. Patricia was presented with a silver bowl. But I would like to read to you what a Scottish newspaper wrote about them on their completion of 20 years service to SYHA. It talked of Dennis in his early years, working for the cotton mills, with youth organisations, and as a choirmaster and Sunday School teacher. It went on to say this: 'Since then the couple have catered for more than 16,000 visitors a year to the Glenmore hostel, which is open all year round. In addition, Dennis has instituted various courses, while Patricia has won accolades for her cuisine. Visitors say she's the best youth hostel cook in Britain, said Dennis.' I might also add, 'And so say all of us' I think." The guests nodded their approval with enthusiasm.

"That same newspaper also referred to them as: 'The happiest couple in Britain.' And so they were, and that is exactly how we shall always remember them."

The Happy Hostellers; Their Tales.

I had no sooner settled down with my guests than, much to our surprise, we heard the loud ring of the warden's office bell. Amid much laughter someone said "John, I really think you had better go and see who that is."

I wandered slowly through the kitchen and into the hall. I could not help but recall how my uncle might have reacted in the same situation. If we only had eight beds left, and this was a party of ten that he had taken the booking for, his eyes would sparkle and widen, and with a smile he would exclaim, "Fraught, isn't it?" If, on the other hand, it was someone whom he had identified as possible trouble, or if indeed they had innocently interupted a particularly fraught moment at Canasta, then he would quote from his favourite poem, Lord Macaulay's 'Horatius'. Often, when looking out towards the mountains he would quote: 'On the low hills to the westward, the Consul fixed his eye'; but at a moment such as this he would quote from two stanzas further on: 'But the Consul's brow was sad, and the Consul's speech was low, and darkly looked he at the wall, and darkly at the foe!'.

On reaching the hall I was given a cheerful greeting by twelve smiling faces. I could not help but notice that each of them had removed their boots and had left them in the porch by the front door!

"John" they exclaimed, "We too have come here today in order to tell you some of our tales, and the tales of others who stayed at this youth hostel during the years that your aunt and uncle were here. But first of all we would ask you, if we may, if you would please sit on 'your' windowsill seat, because that is where all of us remember seeing you most, either handing out ski passes, or giving out duties, but perhaps most of all just telling us stories."

"I shall indeed be honoured to do just that" I replied, "and it is a lovely surprise to see you all again; you are all most welcome."

"We remember that you took us out on walks, up and along the forest tracks if it was too windy to ski, or on the track to the Green Loch on summer evenings, or down to the beach on nights of magic when the snow lay deep and crunched under your boots, to gaze with us across a frozen Loch Morlich towards the ghostly white peaks of the Cairngorms." said one of the boys.

"And talking of ghosts" said one of the girls, "that was a story which made quite a few of us a little bit nervous at bedtime!"

I laughed. "I suppose you mean Margaret? Well, this I can promise you is the truth: Just to the east of Cairngorm summit there is a hollow, or small coire. It is popular with snow-holers, skiers, and walkers, a very fine lunch spot with a great view and away from the hordes on Cairngorm. Its name, in Gaelic, is 'Ciste Mhearad', which means 'Margaret's Coffin!' Now, there are several legends connecting this with Clan Grant and Clan McIntosh of Moy. Of these I know very little. But I was told this: Margaret worked as a servant girl here in this building when it was a shooting lodge. She may once have arranged to meet a young McIntosh on top of Cairngorm, or so the story goes. Quite romantic I suppose, except that he stood her up! She is supposed to have wandered around the summit, presumably heartbroken, and eventually succumed to the cold and died in the place which bears her name."

Everybody had gone quiet. "Whether she returned to her place of work or not I cannot say. The few stories I have heard do not so much involve a lady in white walking through a wall, but more of footsteps, and doors opening and shutting, which on stormy nights is enough to un-nerve anybody. The only thing which I cannot reasonably explain is that two 'hard men' climbers from Dundee, having booked to stay for four nights, suddenly packed up and left after the first night, looking scared and only muttered something about a cupboard door opening, hearing someone walking into it and then the door closed again."

Very soon we were laughing and chatting again; this was after all a gathering of old friends. I got down from my windowsill and sat on the floor. The rest followed my lead and sat around in a semicircle, ready to relate their tales. "I have quite a few stories to tell of people who came in the early days" said one of the boys.

"Ian and Margaret came in the days before the ski lifts or the road were built. They and their climbing friends walked 'in a bee-line' across rough heather land up to Cairngorm summit. There were nowhere near as many trees then as now, and they remember with some regret that their climbing equipment was much heavier than todays lightweight gear. Ian still has his wooden-shafted ice axe. They walked several times through the Lairig Ghru, and Ian remembers one cold night in Corrour Bothy when he boiled a kettle with a screw cap and used it as a hot water bottle.

As for the hostel, the dormitories were strictly segregated, even for married couples, and the wardens would not allow anyone outside until they had fulfilled their allocated chores for the day. This was also a time before cooked meals were available, but they did not mind that, being able to use the members kitchen made their holiday affordable."

"Ralph came to the City of Manchester along with many other Jews in 1939. After the war he worked in the textile industry for a while. That is rather similar to what happened to Dennis's father, isn't it John?"

"They had much in common" I replied, "Ralph came to Cheetham Hill and worked in a knitting factory, 12 hour night shifts for 30 shillings a week! He brought his two daughters up to Loch Morlich for the first time when the building was Glenmore Lodge, and they walked half way up Cairngorm and sat to watch them building the ski road. Their second visit was after it became a youth hostel, but they had to hire their skis from Aviemore. Their next visit was momentous. They made friends with Dennis, but that was the week when the ski room burned down. What Ralph remembers most is the length of time it took before the fire brigade from Kingussie arrived, and that the ski room was mostly destroyed by then. They had stored their own skis in the dormitory, and went ski-ing the next day. Ralph and his daughters continued to visit Glenmore for the next 15 years, and became close friends." I smiled. "One particular night, the girls were back a little while after the doors were locked. Dennis let them in with a smile because of who they were and because he wanted to help Ralph with their education - their Mum died when they were young."

"Peter was another who first came here when it was Glenmore Lodge" said one of the girls, "he came on a climbing course. He next came in July 1964 with a group of four friends, all packed into an A30 converted van. They stayed one night at the hostel and then spent the next two nights sleeping at the Shelter Stone by Loch Avon, taking on some hard climbing during the day. On returning to the hostel they met a group of 11 Army cadets who were setting out for the Shelter Stone, and Peter and his friends drove on to Skye laughing at the thought of that number trying to stay in that cramped space. He came next on a hostel ski course and had great fun with Plum as his mentor. The next year he returned, bringing with him his girl friend, who soon became his wife. They gained enough confidence from Plum that they went ski-ing abroad after that, but the couple returned to the hostel twice more for some summer walking. That I know is how Dennis and Patricia built up the legend here, by folk returning again and again, both for the hospitality and for the sheer magic of Glenmore, Loch Morlich, and the mountains."

"Rolf and Viv came from Devon" said another of the boys, "they came on a Christmas ski course but were unlucky with the weather, which they themselves described as, 'appaling'. What little snow there was had been packed into hard ice by the wind - conditions which many folk will remember with some sympathy for these two. Nevertheless they thought that the instructors were a good-natured bunch, and remember one telling them that the previous year he had attempted to climb Everest with a friend, intending to use only the equipment abandoned by previous expeditions. They never made it!

The ski course resorted to the dry slope at Glenmore Lodge. At lunchtime the instructor told them they could stay on the slope provided that there were at least two of them, and promptly disappeared. Whereupon Rolf, dauntless, clambered right to the top of the slope and pointed his skis downwards, little caring that he had no idea how to control speed or stop. He reached the bottom of the slope safely, but at some speed, and glided gracefully through the heather and finished up wrapped around a fence, 'which had been put there to protect a little pond from the likes of me'. The instructor returned, beamed at them and said, 'Don't break a leg on the first day; save it for the end of the week'!"

"Barbara brought her family up to the hostel for a summer holiday. On the first day they went down to the beach and the two children spent a happy hour or two making a sand dam on the small stream which flows into the loch near the road (I must confess I have spent some enjoyable time doing the same thing). Some time later two ladies came and sat down on the beach. They had just made themselves comfortable when the dam, which had been very well made, broke and the ladies, their beach towels and their picnic suddenly found themselves awash. Barbara perhaps should have regarded that as a portent. Two days later there came torrential rain and a flash flood. They heard a rumble of boulders in the river up the hill, and suddenly the bridge was washed away along with a section of the road. Seven or eight cars were stranded above it until help could be found. They drove towards Aviemore and discovered that the same thing had happened just further down the road from the clay pigeon shooting, and they saw that Bella the milk lady's van had almost disappeared into the gap. Perhaps their holiday was saved on their last day when, returning to the beach, they were able to enjoy the awesome sight of an osprey diving to take a fish from the loch."

"Of course" I said, "my friends from school and university came here for holidays too. Andrew came summer and winter. One Hogmanay I took him out to see a few of my friends in Aviemore. On New Years Day Andrew was not very well. Now you guys will probably say that is not unusual, but after two or three days we took the decision that it was possibly not a hangover. D and P moved him into a room upstairs and looked after him for two weeks, until he had recovered from the glandular fever and was able to travel home. In those days, Andrew learned to ski with lace-up leather ski boots, and although most of you had a better start than that, I can tell you that Andrew's family have for many years enjoyed ski holidays abroad.

In the school summer holidays we would play football, either on the beach or using the old front door as a goal, which earned the mild disapproval of the warden. We also devised a 'hostel traverse', by which we would attempt to cross the entire front of the hostel without touching the ground; this heroic mountaineering drew not a few dark looks from Dennis, which had more to do with our technique, or lack of it, than possible damage to the hostel! Andrew and I agree now that as we took on long walks over Cairngorm and the Northern Corries, Braeriach and Cairn Toul, and Ben Macdui, going on to look out over Coire Sputan Dearg, it always seemed to be warm and sunny!"

"It is peculiar" said one of the girls, "that summer memories are always of hot and sunny days, yet those who were here in the depths of winter remember the wildest stormy days best."

"I am sure that is true" I said. "By the time I was at university, I was with friends who shared an interest in military history, so although Chris, Andy and Keith came primarily for ski-ing, we found time to visit Culloden and Ruthven Barracks. You may or may not believe this, but once, on the anniversary of the Battle of Culloden, April 16, we camped on the battlefield, next to the Well of the Dead! University mentality was and is a hard thing to understand; we relied on a bottle of Drambuie to give us courage. Andy is another who now enjoys ski holidays abroad, despite two of his weeks here being when conditions on the hill were very icy indeed."

"I have to say here that I owe a great debt to all the hostel instructors and to my uncle and aunt, in that they always readily accepted my friends as their friends, and all of them would acknowledge that today.

I am sure indeed that the hand of friendship was offered to all of you, as you returned to visit the old homestead on second and subsequent occasions."

"That is absolutely true, John" said another of the girls, "and that is why we are more than happy to join you this day in your great feast, and to tell our stories."

"Talking of which" said another, "there were some skier groups who came a few times but were not part of the ski course, because they could all ski competently, in some cases very well indeed. The group from the Steeple church in Dundee styled themselves, 'The Zambian Freestyle Ski Team', and Dennis would take some delight when 'The Dollar Dollies' would return for another year. The 'Rockhoppers' of course, are now legend; two who had connections with that group were Jo and Clare. They were in Plum's class to begin with, and it was one of those weeks when the snow conditions were OK, but on the Saturday when it was time to go home, then the snow really fell, (how often did that happen?) and from that a life-long friendship developed. Jo well remembers a New Year's holiday which was warm enough to walk around Loch Morlich in t-shirts, yet she will always remain a fanatical skier, just as her mum and dad were. She tried again the following New Year and the snow was unbelievable! Jo would travel up from Plymouth in the early days, and has scary memories of sitting on Crewe station at midnight, thinking of the film 'Ghost Train'."

"That was at a time when 'The Stingrays' would entertain folk in Aviemore" I said, " I think that most of you might remember them, or 'The Trampies'."

"Fantastic entertainment both of them" said one of the boys, "but remember our priority was always to get back up the road in time for lights out! I am sure both those groups could easily identify the youth hostel crowd, the ones who always left early, and usually in a great hurry."

"Rosemary and Kay came over by boat from Australia, and came on a ski course anxious to see snow for the first time! Gordon the instructor gave the course a talk at dinner on the Saturday. They remember Walter being very patient with them and teaching them well, and on the last day they took part in one of Plum's terrifying routes home, through the forest, and the girls abiding memory is of colliding with so many pine trees they thought there would be no forest left, yet they still think it was great fun."

"And so say all of us" said a girl, "Plum would take us all up to the top of Coire na Ciste, ski along the east ridge and sometimes into Coire Laoigh Mhor, we would come swooping out with enough speed to carry us all the way to the road. Then the fun began, following a steep and narrow path down through the trees, grabbing hold of one was often the best way to stop."

"Happy days" I said. "Such were the memories of two Australians, I am not sure they were too impressed with cold showers and bunk beds, but they very much enjoyed the food and the whole experience. The photo I have shows Cairngorm with a very sparse covering of snow; if you will forgive me for talking of ourselves, this shows how hard we had to work sometimes to keep everybody ski-ing."

"Karen and Jane were members of that noble band of folk who spent their first day in the calm shelter of the Hayfield. There we worked you hard, to prepare you for going into the big wide world of T-Bars and Pomas the next day! Karen's anorak was made by her dad, who was reluctant to invest in ski gear until he was sure that his daughter would enjoy the sport. Quite a responsibilty for us, but Karen now takes her own children ski-ing. Jane was yet another member of the Loch Morlich marriage bureau; after the course she moved from Sheffield to London to be nearer to Andy; they are now living happily ever after in Cumbria. Karen returned a few times, ski-ing sometimes in the forest and sometimes on the mountain, but she did not seem to mind. What she certainly remembers is racing back from Aviemore before the doors would be locked!"

"Fiona, Rebecca and Jessica came on a ski course and made it their business to keep everyone in fits of laughter for the whole week. They were enthusiastic participants in the Friday night ceilidh, during which they performed a song which they had composed about the week's events, which incidentally had been brilliant ski-ing. That song owes something to the Beatles' 'Let It Be' and I am happy to tell you (not sing!) a small part of it now."

> 'When I find myself in times of trouble
> Skiing down the Aonach
> leaping over moguls
> Let us ski, let us ski.

Let us ski (4 times)
Skiing in the Cairngorms
Let us ski, let us ski

When I'm skiing down the White Lady
Plum is skiing behind me
Shouting words of wisdom
Bend ze knees, bend ze knees

When she leaves the kitchen in the morning
Liz leaves the porridge far behind
Exchanging spoons for skis, spoons for skis.'

"I think we displayed some hidden talents at your ceilidhs, John" said a boy, "I was there when a group of Morris men were on the course, phenominally fit guys, and they taught us a couple of really good folk dances."

"The 'Edinburgh Crowd' are all definitely agreed on one thing: as they will tell you, 'If you can ski in Scotland you can ski anywhere'. They can certainly prove that because since youth hostel days they have skied in the Pyrenees, the Alps, France, Austria, Italy, Switzerland, Utah and Colorado. This may be because what they remember about Scotland is being lashed by a snow storm on a ski lift, turning to each other and agreeing that they were definitely off their rockers, being completely blown off the poma by 90 mph winds, and, well I can sum it up for you by quoting a verse from a song which they performed at a ceilidh:

'Now I want to go to Heaven
With Marion's class
'cause Marion's class
can ski on glass'!

"Who were they, 'The Edinburgh Crowd', John?" asked one of the girls.

"Ah, now let me see" I said, "Naomi, Melanie, two Alisons (at least), Shelagh, Mary, Karen, George, Kevin, and Eamonn, and I hope they forgive me if I have forgotten anyone. And of course they did not ski only in the bad times. Melanie's first instructor was Anna Cook, and that year they skied into June. Many happy times on the slopes followed. All of them enjoyed the camaraderie, not only with each other but with the instructors and with Dennis and Patricia. All of them remain hooked on ski-ing to this day. Straight after ski-ing they would all head down to Glenmore Shop for the hot apple strudel and ice cream. After dinner it would be down to the 'Dip 'n' Disco' at the Coylumbridge, enjoying the comparative luxury of the hotel and dancing for as long as their legs would carry them. They were once even able to charm the local Police after they were stopped for 'slaloming' down the road back to the hostel!

And, after all, Melanie and Kevin, Karen and Eamonn provided two more entries in the Loch Morlich marriage book!"

"Perhaps the best entry in that book should belong to Jane and Ian" said another of the girls. "They had each visited the hostel a couple of times seperately, but in February 1980 they were in your class, John. I think you remember that as a rather special class, everyone got on well and the week was just perfect. Trips down to Coylumbridge became a contest to discover how many hostellers would fit into a bright orange Beetle! When it came time to go home Ian drove down to Aviemore station to see Jane and Julie off on the train to London. When their train arrived in Stirling, there was Ian on the station platform, and he presented the girls with spare ribs from KFC. Not bad for a Beetle! Ian then went to London to see Jane at Great Ormond Street, and soon after they tried to book the hostel together for a few days. They were fully booked, but Jane phoned Dennis (aka Cupid in her words) and of course he used his elastic hostel to fit them in. No doubt he described it as 'fraught'. Visits to parents followed, and in January 1981 Ian and Jane became engaged, and they married in October of the same year in Somerset."

At that very moment a loud female voice, with a recognisable Queensland accent came from the dining room: "Your soup's on the table - come and get it then"

And what a glorious feast we all enjoyed at the end of that memorable day.

Epilogue

It briefly crossed my mind to end the book with these words: 'Here taketh the makere of this book his leve', but I have already taken quite enough liberties with Chaucer by 'borrowing' his great idea of a group of travellers telling their tales. I hope he will forgive me and I further hope that you, gentle reader, will think of it as an appropriate method of relating what happened over all those years in the building which I always knew as Loch Morlich Youth Hostel.

Acknowldgements here must of necessity be all-embracing. To each and every member of staff, and to each and every hosteller I offer my deep gratitude. Because I was there over so many years there will inevitably be some whose names and deeds I have forgotten to record; I seek their forgiveness.

I will take this opportunity to record my debt of gratitude to two men. To Jim Martin, General Secretary SYHA during most of my time there, for the trust which he placed in me and the opportunities he gave me to explore the wider world of Scottish hostels. And to Plum Worral, for his infinte patience with me, and for sharing some of the secrets of his gift of perfect balance with me. Whatever was good about my own style of teaching, I owe it to that great man.

I was of course constantly aware that I held a 'priveledged' position as a family member when working alongside other members of staff, but as far as I know no-one at all ever resented that, and for their kindness towards me I remain humbly grateful.

If anyone deserves special acknowledgement then it must be the following people:

138

Lorentz Äge, whose father was an Officer in Kompani Linge and in whose possession was their wartime logbook.

John Martin, SYHA's archivist. We exchanged information about Loch Morlich and other hostels, and he so very kindly digitised the famous hostel slide-show for me.

Last but by no means least, dear Phil and Gaile Sanderson, who took over the reins so gracefully when my family left, and who then began to make their own book of stories. Their tale is yet to be told, and I hope that one day it will be.